NEW MEXICO CHILES

HISTORY, LEGEND *and* LORE

KELLY URIG
ILLUSTRATIONS BY LIZ BUCKLER

AMERICAN PALATE

Published by American Palate
A Division of The History Press
Charleston, SC 29403
www.historypress.net

Front cover, top right: Courtesy of the New Mexico State University Library, Archives and Special Collections. *Bottom right:* Courtesy of Chris Biad, the Hatch Chile Store.

All images are courtesy of the author unless otherwise noted.

First published 2015

Manufactured in the United States

ISBN 978.1.62619.864.7

Library of Congress Control Number: 2015939215

Notice: The information in this book is true and complete to the best of our knowledge. It is offered without guarantee on the part of the author or The History Press. The author and The History Press disclaim all liability in connection with the use of this book.

This book is dedicated to my family, whom I love more than food, more than chile.

CONTENTS

CONTENTS

FOREWORD

Believe it or not, Kelly Urig didn't particularly like to eat chile peppers when she was growing up in Santa Fe, New Mexico. But she was immersed in the chile pepper culture of a family and extended family that grew chiles and other crops in the southern part of New Mexico near Hatch and Salem. Every two years, that extended family would throw a reunion in an onion shed at their farm in Salem, and the primary goal of that get-together of roughly eighty chile lovers was to make red chile sauce—lots of red chile sauce. Gradually, Kelly grew to accept the sauce and finally became a convert to the hot stuff.

Fast-forward several years and Kelly is working on her master's degree in filmmaking at San Diego State University, and she's looking for a thesis subject. In film school, this means two things: writing and producing a film and then writing a thesis about exactly how the film was made.

Naturally, she chose chile peppers as the subject of her thesis, and rather than producing a how-to film about cooking, she chose to reveal what chile peppers mean to the identity and culture of New Mexicans. Like Arturo Lomelí and me, she knew that chiles were more than just food. "Chile, they say, is the king, the soul of the Mexicans," wrote Lomelí in *El Chile y Otros Picantes* (1986), "a nutrient, a medicine, a drug, a comfort. For many Mexicans, if it were not for the existence of chile, their national identity would begin to disappear." And since Nuevo Mexico was once the northernmost province of the newly independent Estados Unidos Mexicanos, Lomelí's chile sentiment applies to New Mexicans, too. Kelly writes that chile is "the red and green blood of New Mexico."

So Kelly wrote, produced and directed the award-winning, twenty-six-minute production called *The Chile Film*, defended her thesis and received her master's degree. Then, with the assistance of Ann Lerner, film liaison officer for the City of Albuquerque, Kelly obtained entry-level jobs in the film industry, working in the accounting department of the Johnny Depp movie *Transcendence* and in the costume department of the television production *Longmire*.

Then Kelly got a call from an editor asking the question, "We know you can make a movie about chile peppers, but can you write a book about them?" This volume indicates that, indeed, she can.

"Chile gives people so much joy," Kelly told me when I asked her what fascinates her the most about chile peppers. "When I first learned that eating chiles makes your body release endorphins, I realized how multidimensional they are."

And like me, Kelly is now addicted to chile peppers—and not just to eating them but to writing about them, too.

DAVE DEWITT

PREFACE

Since I can remember, chile has been a part of my life and a huge part of my family's traditions. However, I wasn't always a fan of chile. For the first decade of my life, it seemed that I was the only child in my entire family that requested "chile on the side" or—heaven forbid—"mild chile." I would get the loving yet teasing remarks from several of my family members as they declared, "How can you be a member of this family?" or "Are you a *real* New Mexican?"

I can't remember the first time I tasted chile, but I can remember when my attitude toward it changed. I ordered a breakfast burrito smothered in green chile from Tecolote Café (a Sunday morning breakfast favorite of our family for many years). It was the first time I did not ask for chile on the side. My parents' eyes widened as if to say, "Are you sure you can handle it?" To everyone's surprise—even my own—I did handle it. It took many more years and moving away from New Mexico to discover what was so significant about chile to New Mexicans and to gain a better understanding of my cultural identity. In a manner of speaking, chile found me and led me back home to where it all started: family and our traditions of farming and making the best chile.

New Mexico is called the "Land of Enchantment," and its enchanting magic is what this is all about, but it can be easy to overlook. The magic of New Mexico isn't just the breathtaking landscapes where the sky touches the earth in every direction and whose vastness evokes a feeling of limitless possibility. The magic of New Mexico isn't the sunrises and sunsets that contain every shade of the rainbow—and some you didn't even know existed—or the vibrant gold, orange and red fall colors that spread across our beautiful mountain ranges. The magic of New Mexico isn't just our little brown adobe houses that honor our wide-open landscapes. The magic of New Mexico isn't the thousands of hot-air balloons that fill the sky and land in backyards or streets or the snowy winters when the aroma of piñon wood fireplaces fills the brisk air. The magic of New Mexico isn't just our wildflowers that come alive with the slightest drop of rain as if to say thank you for that one small bit of water. The magic of New Mexico isn't just the free entertainment of our thunder and lightning that lights up the darkest of nights. The magic of New Mexico isn't just in the lives and personalities of our mesas, those centuries-old formations in which secrets of the earth, history and our ancestors are held.

The magic of New Mexico is our diverse people, our history and our traditions. The magic of New Mexico is chile.

ACKNOWLEDGEMENTS

Thank you to the many people, organizations, restaurants, farms, cafés and chocolatiers that participated in the making of this book:

Archuleta family
Kassie Asel
Biad Family Farms
Bueno Foods, Ana Baca
Café Pasqual's, Katharine Kagel
Chile Pepper Institute, Dr. Paul Bosland, Danise Coon and Dr. Stephanie Walker
ChocolateSmith, Kari and Jeff Keenan
Jessica Clark
Coyote Café and Cantina, Eric DiStefano
Paige Davidson
James Ditmore, aka the "Chile Whisperer"
El Pinto Restaurant, Jim and John Thomas and Douglas Evilsizor
Franzoy family, Doris and Bobby
Harry's Roadhouse, Harry Shapiro and Peyton Young
Hatch Chile Express LLC
Hatch Chile Festival
Hatch Chile Sales, Preston and Elaine Mitchell
Heidi's Organic Jams, Heidi Eleftheriou
C.G. Higgins
Jubilations Wine and Spirits Store
Kakawa, Tony Bennett

ACKNOWLEDGEMENTS

La Choza and the Shed Restaurants, Carswell family, Courtney, Josh and Sarah
Laguna Pueblo
Leona's Resteraunte de Chimayó, Dennis Tiede and family
Blanche Leone
Los Chileros, Chuck Waghorne and Ian Johnson
Los Poblanos Historic Inn and Organic Farm
Al Lucero
Jimmy and Faron Lytle and June Rutherford
NMSU Library Archives and Special Collections Department
New Mexico Chile Association
New Mexico Department of Agriculture, Katie Goetz
Marcia Nordyke
Old Pecos Foods, Mike and Dianne Jaramillo
Carmella Padilla
Project Mainstreet Las Cruces Chile Drop, Marissa Coronado and Russ Smith
Matt Romero
Santa Fe Farmer's Market
Santa Fe School of Cooking, Susan Curtis, Nicole Curtis Ammerman and
    Noe Cano
Santa Fe Wine and Chile Fiesta
Señor Murphy's
José and Antonio de Serrano
Sichler family, John, Elenor, Tim and Naomi
Tea Chileño, William Zunkel
Tia Sophia's, Nick Maryol
Todos Santos, Hayward Simoneaux
Tomasita's Restaurant, George Gundry and Georgia Maryol
Tourism Santa Fe
Town of Red River, Hot Chile Days and Cool Mountain Nights
Sarah Traux
Whole Enchilada Fiesta
Young Guns Produce, Adam Franzoy

Very special thanks to:

Berridge family
Liz Buckler
Matt Culler
Dave DeWitt
Christen Thompson

CHILE DISCLAIMER

I am not a chef, horticulturalist, scientist of any kind, farmer or restaurateur. I don't claim to know everything there is to know about chile because I am always learning more every day. I don't claim to have eaten at every New Mexican restaurant in the state or to have tasted even half of their dishes—maybe not even a quarter—but I am still trying. I am just a "Chile Chica" who loves eating #chileeverydamnday and am proud to share my culture with everyone.

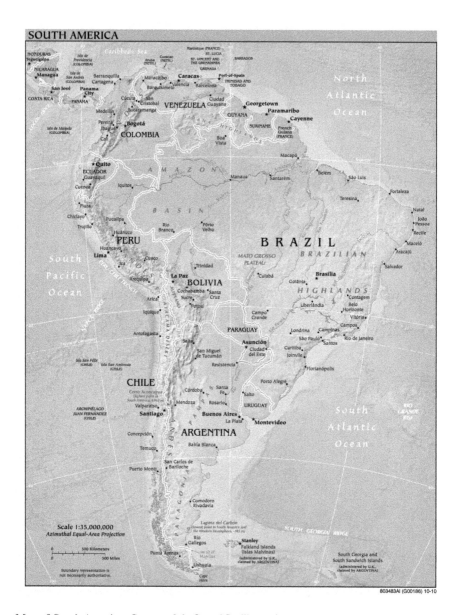

803483AI (G00186) 10-10

Map of South America. *Courtesy of the Central Intelligence Agency.*

Part I
AN INTRODUCTION TO CHILE

HISTORY OF CHILE: JOURNEY INTO THE HEART OF NEW MEXICAN CULTURE

The Origins of Chile

To understand the cultural impact chile has had on New Mexican life, we need to begin with the origins of chile. Research proves that all chiles originated in the western hemisphere, and popular belief specifies South America near the modern-day Bolivia nuclear region, which includes portions of neighboring Peru, Brazil and Paraguay. This is significant because some of the most popular cuisines in the world that include chile in many of their dishes (i.e. Chinese, Thai, Indian) did not have chile until the "discovery" of the New World. Once introduced, chile changed the entire construct and diet of these cultures around the world.

We really need to thank birds in a big way for spreading wild chiles around South and Central America. Birds don't possess capsicum receptors, so they don't taste heat (something I will explain in much more detail in "Science of Chile"), and their digestive systems do not process the seeds. These small peppers they pick up are used for nesting purposes, all the while making it easier for the seeds to fertilize and grow in new regions.

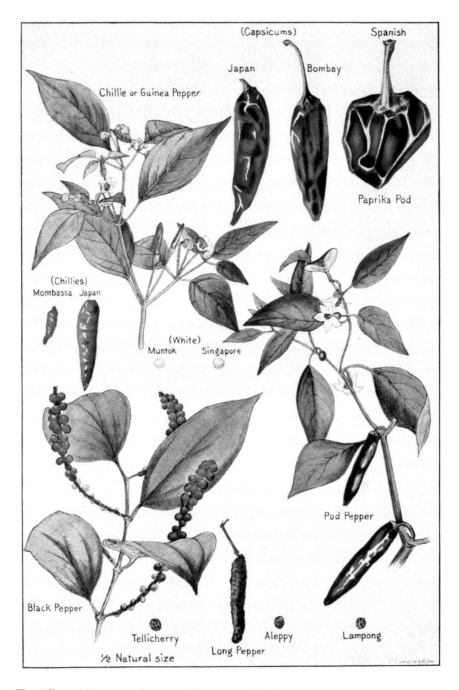

The difference in anatomy between chile peppers (*Capsicum annuum*) and pepper (*Piperaceae*). *From* Spices, Their Nature and Growth, and the Vanilla Bean *(Baltimore, MD: McCormick and Co., 1915)*.

Botanically speaking, chiles are considered berries. The original peppers resembled small berries and were nowhere near the size that can be grown today. The chiltepin, a perennial shrub also known as the "bird pepper," grows wild and can live as long as fifty years in some places. It has small, bright red, berry-sized peppers that would have been appealing to birds. Today, there are thousands of varieties of chile peppers, including over thirty different wild species and five species of domesticated chile peppers.

So who domesticated chiles first? We really don't have a definitive answer to that question, but it is known that chiles have been part of the diet of people in the Americas for thousands of years. Archaeologist R.S. MacNeish discovered chile seeds at his excavations in Tamaulupas and Tehuacan. MacNeish's findings, compounded with the discovery of a whole chile pod in the Guitarrero Cave in Peru dated to 6500 BC, indicate that chile peppers were cultivated as far back as ten thousand years ago. The chile pod found in the Guitarrero Cave was most likely a wild pepper rather than one that was domesticated. The native people of Mexico, Central America and part of South America were the first to domesticate chile crops. Experts today agree that chiles were domesticated by 3300 BC, over five thousand years ago.

A lot of people say that Christopher Columbus "discovered" chile peppers. In actuality, Columbus was just one of the first Europeans to have one of his crew members, Dr. Diego Alvarez Chanca, bring the peppers back to his employers. Columbus wrote in his log on January 15, 1492, about "*aji*," the native people's pepper, "which is more valuable than [black] pepper, and all the people eat nothing else, it being very wholesome. Fifty caravels might be annually loaded with it [from Hispaniola]."

Dr. Diego Alvarez Chanca, a physician on Columbus's second voyage to the West Indies in 1493, brought the first chile peppers to Spain and wrote about their possible medicinal uses. Chile traveled to the Caribbean just as it had spread to South and Central America prior to Columbus's arrival. Within a matter of a few decades, chile had spread all over the world and confused some Europeans who traveled to Asia in search of its origins. Sixteenth-century Spanish explorer Bartolomé de las Casas wrote about Native Americans: "*Sin chile, no creen que están comiendo!*" meaning, "Without chile, they don't believe they are eating!"

Early Trade to New Mexico

According to Dr. Paul Bosland, director of the Chile Pepper Institute at New Mexico State University:

> *By the time Columbus made his voyage, the Aztecs had already developed the jalapeño, poblano, pasilla, serrano, and were using these different chiles in their cuisines and knew what chiles were better for a specific kind of dish. What's really interesting is that each time humans came in contact with chile; they found a use for it and domesticated it. That is why we have five domesticated species.*

The early native peoples of New Mexico were the Mogollons (moggy-YONS) and the Ancestral Puebloans (also known as the Anasazi) from the north. The Pueblo Indians of the Southwest today are direct descendants of prehistoric Indian cultures that built massive stone structures like Chaco Canyon, Mesa Verde and Cedar Mesa hundreds of years before the first recorded Europeans saw North America. Indians of central Mexico, especially the Toltec, influenced the Mogollon and Anasazi people. Many archaeologists today agree on a wide trade network between the Southwest Indians and the Toltec people, commonly exchanging exotic bird feathers, among other items, for turquoise. The Toltec empire fell around AD 1122, later giving rise to the Aztecs. The height of the Aztec empire was around 1486–1502, just before the Spanish arrived. Spanish explorer Hernando Cortés landed on the Gulf of Mexico coast in 1519, allowing the Spanish to work their way farther north into present-day New Mexico. Scientists have found no evidence that chile was in New Mexico prior to the Spanish arrival.

Author Jean Andrews, "the Pepper Lady," notes:

> *Thus capsicums traveled from the New World to the Old and back again to Europe by way of the Orient—all before the arrival of the Pilgrims at Plymouth Rock. During the time required for journey, peoples of Africa, India, the Middle East and the Far East so completely incorporated the new spices into their cookery that each area had developed not only a unique cuisine based on capsicums but also unique peppers not to be found in the Americas today.*

It wasn't until the summer of 1540 (eighty years before the pilgrims arrived on the *Mayflower*) that Spanish explorer Francisco Vázquez de Coronado came north to New Mexico and discovered the cultures of the Pueblo people. Baltasar Obregón, a member of Antonio Espejos's expedition into New Mexico in 1582, wrote, "They have no chile, but the natives were given some to plant." This journal entry is one of the main factors by which historians and archaeologists deduce that chile was not grown in New Mexico prior to Spanish arrival. The Pueblo people of New Mexico have been growing and eating chile as a regular part of their diet for at least four hundred years. Don Juan de Oñate and his men are also credited for bringing chiles into northern New Mexico on their 1598 exploration into San Gabriel del Yunge, near modern-day San Juan Pueblo. Oñate and his settlers claimed Santa Fe the same year, but it did not become the official capital of New Mexico until 1610, under the governorship of Don Pedro de Peralta, making Santa Fe the oldest capital in the United States. During early Spanish settlement of New Mexico, the cultivation of chile spread rapidly. This gave New Mexico distinct food ways that became widely popular and vastly different from early U.S. East Coast diets.

These first varieties of chile grown in New Mexico are also known as "land race" chiles. They grow a medium-sized green pod that turns red in the fall. Today in New Mexico, there are about twenty-three different land race varieties that spread mostly throughout the northern communities. They are known for adapting to the specific climates of locations like Chimayó, Española, Velarde and Dixon, where they are still grown today. Hot summer days and cool nights in a high-altitude desert have provided a specific set of challenges that farmers know all too well. Throughout time,

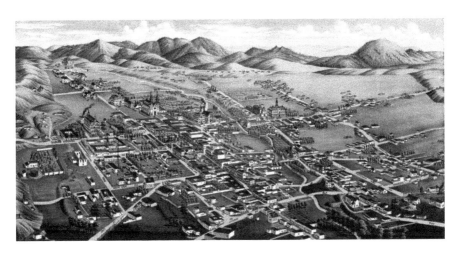

A map from 1882 giving a sense of what Santa Fe once looked like. *Library of Congress, Geography and Map Division.*

Spanish explorer Juan de Oñate, whose exploration is given credit for having brought chiles to New Mexico in the early 1600s.

these chiles have developed a high tolerance to blights, diseases, droughts and other climate factors that can detrimentally affect a harvest.

Chiles in New Mexico were traditionally grown among the three sisters (beans, corn and squash). Today among the Pueblo people of New Mexico, it is still common to see chiles grown among the three sisters.

Chimayó Chile

Many farmers throughout New Mexico still irrigate their crops with water from the Rio Grande, just as the native Pueblo people did hundreds of years ago. For New Mexicans, the chile grown in the northern region has a mystical value in addition to its historical value. Chimayó chile does not grow into a large pod, but it packs a mean punch of heat that is accompanied by an earthy sweetness. How many people in the vast United States can say that when they eat chile, it comes from a seed that has been passed down from their ancestors or early settlers from hundreds of years ago? Today, most of the produce we buy at supermarkets comes from varieties that have been developed as recently as the past decade. With the advent of genetically modified foods, most

Hanging chile ristras for drying on Isleta Pueblo in the 1940s. *Library of Congress, Prints & Photographs Division.*

American diets do not consist of "heirloom" varieties unless you happen to shop regularly at farmers' markets and gourmet grocery stores or grow your own food.

North Versus South

One of the reasons people designate green chile as being from the southern part of the state and red chile as being from the northern portion is because of the shorter season of land race varieties; they turn red more quickly than the southern varieties. In northern New Mexico, it was almost impossible to grow the varieties from down south, like NuMex No. 9. However, today you can see the Heritage NuMex Big Jim variety

Antonio de Serrano picks a land race variety the day before a local farmers' market to sell fresh red chile and roast it as purchased.

of chile growing in Española, although it is much more common to see Española Improved, which was bred for the northern climate. Most northern chile farmers plant only on small acreage, as family land has continued to be subdivided over the years and fewer people use the land to farm. All chile needs to be harvested by hand, except for red chile, for which there are newer mechanical ways to harvest the entire plant that sort the pepper from the dead plant. This makes chile in both northern and southern communities a labor-intensive crop to grow.

Southern New Mexico grows more of the chiles that were developed by New Mexico State University (NMSU) to be harvested more commercially as dried, canned or pickled products, in addition to the tradition of roasting and selling by the roadside. Chiles grown in the south are often brought up north to Albuquerque and Santa Fe to be sold. Most New Mexicans would, and still do, get their red chiles from the northern part of the state and their green chiles from Hatch or Mesilla Valley to last them the entire year. In the late 1800s and early 1900s, there were still farms around the Albuquerque area, but they decreased as the city grew.

It is common in New Mexico to overhear a lively debate about where the best chile comes from. I've had the good fortune of tasting countless red and green chiles from all regions of New Mexico, and I would never disagree with a farmer or anyone from Chimayó or Hatch that they have the best chile in the world. My extended family grows chile in the Hatch Valley, but I was raised in the north, so the debate is more personal. When people ask where the best chile comes from, it's as if they are asking me if I have a favorite child. For me, it's not about north versus south and who grows better chile. What matters is that I get my chile from New Mexico and nowhere else. When I buy chile from the supermarket, farmers' market or a roadside stand, I am placing a vote. My vote has always been, and will always be, for New Mexican farmers to continue to do what they love, which is a sacred tradition.

SCIENCE OF CHILE

When you look at the history of chiles and their evolution, it really isn't too surprising that they have become so popular. Studies conducted in the past couple of years have shown that people who eat chiles are more likely to be "risk takers." Chile eating can also help with weight loss, lower blood pressure and even lead to greater team bonding. Chile peppers are cholesterol free, low in sodium and calories and rich in vitamins A and C (one fresh green chile contains more vitamin C than three oranges, and a red chile pod packs more vitamin A than a carrot). They are a good source of folic acid, potassium and vitamin E. Not everyone enjoys eating chiles despite the health benefits, as the spicy factor scares some away. So why are some people hooked on chiles?

Humans enjoy a thrill. We love going to haunted houses and scary movies, riding roller coasters and being frightened for the sake of it, knowing that we will not experience any physical harm. Eating chiles is similar. Most of us know that we will experience some sort of heat when we eat chiles—for many people this is painful and the reason they stay away from anything spicy—but for chile consumers, it is the high that keeps us coming back for more.

When we consume chiles, capsaicinoids (molecules that create heat in peppers) connect to the TRPV1 pain/heat receptors found in our mouths. The receptors send a chemical messenger, "Substance P," to our brains that we are on fire and in pain. To block the perceived pain, our brains trigger a release of endorphins from the pituitary and hypothalamus glands. This

Chemical reactions produced when chiles enter the human body. A) Neurotransmitters send a message to the brain that the body is on fire, and B) the brain releases endorphins to counter the pain from the B1) pituitary and B2) hypothalamus glands—an addictive quality for many "chile heads."

is the fire department response system in our brains; instead of using water to squash out the heat, our brains send a wave of elating endorphins. The influx of endorphins to the pituitary gland is why most people sweat when eating chile. The release creates a sense of well-being.

The high of endorphins counteracts our perceived experience of pain. With increased frequency of progressively hotter chiles, our bodies develop a pain tolerance, explaining why some chile fanatics will suffer through the pain to reach that oh-so-good endorphin release.

Capsaicin has many common uses other than giving chile heads a high. It's used as a topical analgesic agent (sore muscle cream) in the treatment of arthritis, shingles, nerve damage and migraines. Mayans even used to spread chile powder on their gums to ease the pain of toothaches. Oleoresin, the natural resin found in red chile pods, is used to color a variety of cosmetics like red lipstick, as well as a number of colored food products.

While there are many enjoyable uses for chiles today, it is reassuring to know the peppers are not actually addictive. It's the high of endorphins to which people perceive they are addicted, very similar to a "runner's high." Chiles are by far one of the safest "addictions" to have. They are packed full of healthy vitamins and have no lingering side effects. Ask any chile aficionado—like myself—if chile withdrawal is a real thing, and the answer will be yes. I always keep a shaker of dried red chile in my purse, as well as some sort of hot sauce. You never know when those chile cravings are going to rear their ugly heads. Better to be safe than sorry.

Dr. Bosland, director of the Chile Pepper Institute, has developed a five-part test for the heat profile of a chile. The test is an example of all the different variations the taste of a pepper can have and how they differ by person. Each individual has his or her own unique set of taste preferences. Some taste preferences are results of foods we are exposed to, memories (good or bad) in relationship to those foods and our own unique palates. Flavor preferences are as complex and dynamic as each individual; no one is exactly the same. However, differentiating each person's sensitivity to chile *is*, and Dr. Bosland's test for the heat flavor of a chile is fun to try with

---

Chile Chica Pro Tip

If you are not a fan of spicy foods and you happen to experience an adverse reaction to some spicy chile, DO NOT DRINK WATER. Take it from someone who won second place at the Hatch Chile Festival green chile–eating contest, where, after eating twelve extremely hot XX Lumbre chiles, I downed a bottle of water, which only spread the capsaicin oil like wildfire. Holy inferno! It felt like I had poured lava into my intestines. Milk, on the other hand, or any dairy product that contains casein (a fat-loving protein), easily binds to the oily capsaicin and will help wash it down with minimal pain.

a group of people. Invite over some friends and family members, prepare an assortment of chile peppers and ask your guests to write down their responses to these five questions: 1) How rapidly does the heat develop? Is it instantaneous, or is the heat delayed? 2) How long does the heat linger? Does it dissipate quickly? 3) Is the heat sharp or flat? Does it feel like pins poking you in the mouth, or does it feel like a painted, flat heat? 4) Where do you sense the heat? Do you feel it on the tip of the tongue or on the back of the palate? 5) Do you consider the heat level mild, medium or hot? Because each person responds differently to chile heat and the flavor of a pepper, it is a fun experiment to see where other people's preferences lie.

Wilbur Scoville and the Scoville Heat Unit

In 1912, American pharmacist Wilbur Scoville developed a heat-measuring test that relied on measurements of heat from zero to sixteen million (which is pure capsaicin). He would extract the capsaicin from a pepper and dilute it in a mixture of sugar water until a taste tester no longer detected heat. He named the values of his test Scoville Heat Units (SHU), and they are the mostly widely known metrics to measure heat in use today. Every new dilution increased the number on the SHU; for example, the New Mexican Anaheim pepper ranks anywhere from five hundred to five thousand on the SHU. This means it had to be diluted five hundred to five thousand times depending on the taste tester's subjectivity. The general knowledge of the test and its popularity are the reason so many hot sauce companies still use it today. More accurate methods have been developed, such as the High Performance Liquid Chromatography, which measures the exact amount of capsaicin in a pepper. These extraction techniques are popular with "super hots." Scientists remove a pepper's heat and send it to companies that use diluted capsaicin to spray over potato chips (giving every chip a consistent spicy heat), to infuse into hot sauces or to add to topical creams.

TERROIR—PARDON MY FRENCH

The word *terroir* and its meaning are innate to most New Mexican farmers, and the word describes the core of their work. Terroir was described to me by Parisian chef Aude Barbera as being three things that make a particular food the way it is. Those three things are: the location where the product is grown (geography), the kind of elements and nutrients in the soil (geology) and finally, and perhaps most importantly, the weather (climate). In French and many other European cultures, terroir is talked about often when referring to a particular type of wine, champagne, cheese, olive, tea or tomato—and the list goes on. These three factors are in essence what make a particular type of Roma tomato taste the way it does. The most popular and commonly talked about example is champagne. The eponymous drink legally earns its

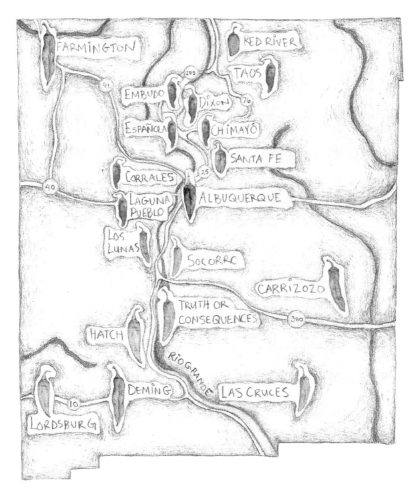

Within New Mexico, many villages, towns and cities grow local land race chiles, as well as NMSU varieties. The Rio Grande is similar to the vein of chiles, supplying water to farms from north to south.

name only if the grapes from which it is made come from the Champagne region of France; all other bubbly wines are given other names: "sparkling wine," "cava" or "espumante," among others. The champagne makers in France knew that when Dom Pérignon first started making champagne, no other place in the world could have a sparkling wine that tasted like champagne because the region where the grapes are grown, its weather and its soil composition is unique to this part of the world. They basically told the rest of the world that whatever product was made in Champagne had its own unique thumbprint; it could not be replicated anywhere else.

So how does all of this relate back to chile? It's the same way Florida oranges are going to taste the way they do only if grown in Florida, or the same way Idaho potatoes have their unique taste or the way that the purist bourbon is made only in Kentucky. Terroir is a very old notion and has been applied to many foods and products throughout the centuries. So when I tell people that the chiles grown in New Mexico are unique and different from any other chiles grown anywhere else in the world, it's because it's true. And it's terroir that makes them unique. If you have ever traveled to New Mexico, it is easy to see that most of New Mexico is a desert. Most people have certain images that come to mind when they think of a desert, and I hope I can change or alter some of those perceptions. It is true that it is dry in New Mexico, and we are always battling drought and praying for rain and snow—yes snow, it does snow here! The northern part of New Mexico is very high in altitude, and that makes for a unique growing situation.

The Rio Grande is our state's main river, running north to south and feeding into many of the farms from Española, Socorro and Hatch to Las Cruces. As the river runs north to south, the altitude changes. In Santa Fe, the altitude is 7,260 feet (more than a mile high, but this isn't as widely known as Denver, the "Mile High City"). The altitude in Hatch drops down to 4,058 feet. That is a huge difference! All of this information should be taken into account when considering the different types of chile grown in New Mexico. Locals know that the chile grown in the northern region from Chimayó, Alcalde, Embudo and Española all share a unique taste, as well as the shape of the pepper. This region is known more for its flavorful red chiles; the pods are usually smaller than the varieties grown in the south and typically aren't as thick. Green chiles from the north are not used as much in dishes like chile rellenos. Chiles from the north, when mature, are put outside to dry, made into ristras or dried in some other manner and then pounded down into a chile powder.

As a lifelong local born in this region, I can honestly say that my favorite dried red chile comes from the northern region and has a sweet, smoky flavor. The authentic red chile powder from Chimayó is sold in four-ounce bags with a twenty-dollar price tag. Many people think it's outrageous to see a red chile spice sold for so much and might say things like: "Are the chiles made out of gold?" My answer is: you are paying for a unique product; you are paying for the terroir, among other things. Today, there are extremely few acres of chile actually grown in the Chimayó region. I have a section dedicated to the decline of chile growth in New Mexico, but I will state here that because so few people are farming chile in Chimayó, it makes it very rare—and a rare product comes at a price. Think of Chimayó chile as a type of chile on the endangered food list. This might sound extreme, but this is what is happening. And more people should be concerned because before you know it, this type of land race chile (which is around four hundred years old) might no longer exist.

Chile *not* C-H-I-L-I

We New Mexicans believe that "chile" is the proper way of spelling what we consume and eat daily; "chili" refers to something completely different and sometimes doesn't even contain chile as an ingredient. In New Mexico, when people talk about chile, it can refer to the many ways in which chiles are prepared and served. For example, fresh chopped green chile is called the same thing as green chile that is turned into a sauce. When you go to a restaurant in New Mexico and order a Mexican/New Mexican dish, the server will usually respond with: "Red, green or Christmas?" These questions are in reference to red and green chile sauces that are usually smothered over a particular dish such as an enchilada, burrito, fries, eggs—the list goes on.

In his 1983 statement to the Ninety-eighth Congress, Senator Pete Dominici set the record straight as far as chiles—not chilis—were concerned. He addressed the United States Senate, declaring, "Even the dictionary makes the error." New Mexicans refuse to spell it the way the rest of the United States does. "I nevertheless stand here before the full Senate and, with the backing of my New Mexican constituents, state unequivocally that the dictionary is wrong," Dominici affirmed.

New Mexicans consume mass quantities of this magical and life-giving fruit from birth, and labels on chile products, descriptions of dishes at New

Mexican restaurants and billboards and advertisements all reinforce the fact that chile is spelled with an "e" and not an "i"…I could go on and on about the wonders of red and green chile, but in reality, all I wanted to do was inform Congress on the correct way to spell the word.

Part II
NEW MEXICAN CHILE

A Brief History of Hatch

Hatch, like many towns in New Mexico, did not keep its original name. The original name given by Spanish settlers in 1851 was Santa Barbara, but the Apache (who very likely had their own name for this area) constantly drove out the early settlers from their territory. The area was left vacant for many years until Fort Thorn was established, located about five miles from the village of Santa Barbara. In 1875, General Edward Hatch—the present town's namesake—occupied it. Many years later, in 1928, Hatch became incorporated into the state of New Mexico. Hatch Valley is considered a village in Doña Ana County and comprises six different small farming communities, otherwise known as *colonias*. They are: Garfield, Milagro, Placitas, Rincon, Rodey and Salem. The valley stretches from Caballo Lake down to Tonuco Mountain and is bordered on either side by the mesa lands. This area of New Mexico has long been known for its fertile properties, due in part to its access to the Rio Grande. Since it was established, farmers have grown cotton, corn and onions, but none of these crops is as famous as its chiles.

In 2011, when I was traveling around the state filming my documentary about chile in New Mexico, I met Alex Franzoy. One of ten children born to Celestina and Joseph Franzoy, Alex and his family were among the first settlers in Salem, New Mexico, in the early 1920s, occupying a lush sixty acres of land. The handful of families that homesteaded in the valley dwindled over

A decorated "Chile Capital of the World" sign that can be seen close to entering the Hatch Chile Festival, hosted at the town's municipal airport.

time as many of them sold their properties and moved to other states. The Franzoy family is the only one on record that has continued to stay and farm, expanding their original homestead. The legacy that Joseph and Celestina began is prevalent in Hatch—almost everyone in the valley is related to the Franzoys in some way. The Franzoys have married into the Biad, Gillis, Adams, Berridge and Carson families (to name a few), and all have a hand in the chile industry. Although many people in Hatch are related, even those who are not are treated like family.

When I interviewed Alex Franzoy, he was just shy of turning 101 years old. I had never encountered someone of his age who was in such good health and so incredibly sharp. He was able to give me a colorful idea of what it was like to grow up in a rural homestead, working long days and nights helping to maintain the crops and livestock. It was his father who started growing and selling chile with their other crops on a larger scale at markets. Fabian Garcia developed the New Mexico No. 9 in the early 1900s, but it wasn't officially released until 1921. Not long after, Joseph Franzoy started growing several acres of chile to sell commercially. (It's possible that Joseph Franzoy met Fabian Garcia, as the chile farming community in southern New Mexico was rather small at this time.) The

Alex Franzoy, at the age of 101, discussed his life in Hatch and how his family is proud to grow and sell chile.

The Franzoy family at their Hatch Valley farm in Salem, 1925. *From left to right, back row*: Erina Emma, Rosa Beatrice, Joseph Carlo Sr., June Louise, Alexander Alfonse and Celestina. *Front row*: Charles Philip, Frank John, Fannie, Fred Louis and Joseph Formolo Jr. *Not pictured*: Albert Louis Franzoy. *Courtesy of Bobby Franzoy.*

Franzoy sons would travel to surrounding towns and sometimes as far as Southern California, where their chiles became very popular.

I asked Alex Franzoy if chiles are what helped him live such a long life, and he replied, "Always be honest and be good to people. I don't lie, I think more people need to be honest and be good to people." Then, after a long pause, he added, "I'm not sure about the chiles; once you eat chiles, though, then you've got an appetite for them. We do grow the best chiles here in Hatch." His answer could not have been more perfect. He passed away the next year. He sister June is the last remaining child of Joseph and Celestina.

June Franzoy married James Lytle, who became known in the valley as "Big Jim" after his son Jimmy was born. Lytle worked with Roy Nakayama, and in 1975, Nakayama released the NuMex Big Jim variety of chile pepper in honor of working with James Lytle on its development. Big Jim has become one of the most popular chiles in the United States. The defining qualities of the Big Jim are its length (average is seven to nine inches), width (average about one to one and half inches), thick meat (perfect for easy roasting and peeling, as well as chile rellenos) and its medium-hot heat. Today, James Lytle's son Jim Lytle and grandson Faron Lytle have

continued the family legacy of growing and developing new breeds of chile. In recent years, the father-son team has developed the "Lumbre" extra-hot variety, as well as several other "legacy" peppers. In 2012, Jimmy Lytle broke his mother June's record of growing the world's largest chile pepper. June's record was a fourteen-inch Big Jim, and Jimmy's was a seventeen-inch-long Big Jim. I was able to see this behemoth chile pepper in all its glory in person at the Hatch Chile Festival in 2012, and it looked as long as a person's limb. All I could think was: that would make one heck of a chile relleno!

Jimmy Lytle at the family home of his mother (June Franzoy) in Hatch.

Uncle Sam holding a green chile outside the well-known Sparky's Barbeque in Hatch is a spectacle popular among posing tourists.

Manuel Grácia stands in front of his colorful Mercado de Chile, where he sells a wide assortment of chile ristras of every color in Hatch, New Mexico.

Chile Chica History Factoid

In the early 1900s, it is believed that a farmer named Emilio Ortega brought New Mexican seeds of chile pods that are longer and turn red in the fall to the Anaheim region of Southern California, where many Hispanics were migrating. The varieties of chiles he brought with him are unknown, but they were most likely land race New Mexican types and not Fabian Garcia's New Mexico No.9. These land race chiles quickly became popular, and people started to name the pod type "Anaheim" after the region where they were now being grown. Today, there is very little chile grown in Anaheim, and what is grown is mostly used in salsas or canned whole. This migration of New Mexico chile peppers is significant because for many years the pod type was called Anaheim. Today, most people refer to the pod type as "New Mexican," which includes popular varieties like Big Jim, Sandia and even Anaheim.

Although Hatch is a small town, a lot has changed over the years. What started off as a marshy valley when the Franzoys arrived in the 1920s has grown into an agricultural center of New Mexico. One would not expect, while driving south on I-25, to see such a large expanse of green farmland in the middle of the desert. While the town, farms and orchards have all grown, one thing has stayed the same: the people. If you come to Hatch, you can expect to meet some of the kindest people around and, of course, taste the best chile there is.

CHILE AND CHICOS:
NATIVE AMERICAN CHILE TRADITION

New Mexico is full of Pueblo festivals happening throughout the year. If you are lucky enough to live or visit New Mexico, going to a Pueblo festival that is open to the public is quite possibly one of the most culturally rich experiences you'll ever have the pleasure to enjoy. You'll take in the music of the drums, the traditional Pueblo dance dress and, of course, Pueblo-style food.

One pueblo's hospitality I have personally experienced is the Laguna Pueblo. The Laguna Pueblo is composed of six different villages, and like the various regions of New Mexico, the way a particular chile dish is cooked can vary from village to village. Some of the key ingredients commonly seen are corn (blue or yellow and in various forms), chile and mutton. Other common ingredients are pumpkin, squash and beans. Almost all Pueblo dishes will contain at least one of these ingredients.

Laguna is about an hour drive west of Albuquerque, and it's worth mentioning that the Laguna Burger—a burger diner attached to a gas station convenience store—serves one of the best green chile cheeseburgers in the state. Whether you decide to take a drive to see the scenery or observe a traditional Pueblo festival, Laguna Burger is 100 percent worth a stop.

A friend of mine introduced me to Blanche Leone, a home cook in the Mesita village of Laguna Pueblo. She and her husband invited me to their home so she could share some of the family recipes, handed down from her mother and grandmother, that she cooks for her family. What a treat! I was thrilled to learn some of her cooking traditions. We started off with a meal she cooks on a typical day for her family: red chile beef stew. What I love

Laguna Burger, located off I-40, is known for its $4.99 + tax green chile cheeseburgers that will be the highlight of any road trip.

Dried red chiles are used throughout the winter season to make red chile sauce and in a variety of dishes.

about cooking with Blanche is that, like my grandmother, she does most of her cooking without a recipe. Most of Blanche's cooking is done from memory and by taste.

The way Blanche taught me is to pour enough vegetable oil to coat the bottom of a cooking pot, bring the heat to medium and then add the diced stew meat. After the meat gets a nice brown coat, add diced cilantro and onions. Then add about one to two cups of water to the mixture. Leave the meat and vegetable mixture on medium until there is a brownish color of broth in the bottom of the pot.

While the meat and vegetable mixture was cooking, Blanche and I worked on preparing the chile sauce. She purchased one bag of dried red chile pods, and then we broke off all the stems and cleaned out the seeds. Warning: if you have never done this before, I suggest wearing some type of gloves while cleaning the pods. Blanche is accustomed to the feeling of heat that capsaicin can have on exposed skin. Even though I have known this feeling my entire life, it is nonetheless uncomfortable when you are trying to cook and your hands are on fire.

Next, Blanche puts a handful of dried chile pods into her blender and then adds a couple cups of boiling water and garlic salt to taste. She adds more pods and more water until the chile turns into a thick, puréed chile sauce. Then she pours the chile sauce into her stew mixture, creating a thick beef chile stew, and lets it simmer for about twenty minutes before serving. The beef stew meat in this recipe is commonly replaced with mutton or rabbit when in

Blanche Leone of the village of Mesita in Laguna Pueblo carefully removes the seeds from the dried pods before boiling and blending them to make a red chile sauce.

season. If after making your chile mixture you want to thicken it but don't have any more chiles, Blanche suggests adding blue or yellow cornmeal to the stew to bring it to the consistency you prefer.

To accompany the red chile stew, Blanche whips up a special "native malt," pronounced Hay-Ya-Nee. She boils about two cups of water and then adds blue cornmeal. When the cornmeal comes to malt-like consistency after about five to ten minutes simmering on medium heat, she serves the drink with a cup of sugar on the side so each individual can make the drink however sweet he or she wants it. For those who are looking for alternatives to sugar, adding honey or agave will have the same effect.

Blanche cooks almost every night for her large family. Most nights, her children and grandchildren will come over for her homemade cooking, which, as Blanche says, will always consist of something with chile. As I leave her home, the smell of her homemade chile stew wafts through the brisk fall air, and I am reminded of the smell of cooking with my grandmother. This is part of what makes New Mexico so unique. The diversity of our people is a lot like the different variations of the same kind of recipe; however you cook your chile dish, with whomever you cook, chile is always incorporated and brings together families of all different walks of life.

To Market! To Market! To Roast Some Chile!

It's a late spring Saturday morning, and the Santa Fe Farmers' Market is bustling with business. Talented street musicians play their hearts out while shoppers fill their reusable shopping bags with the freshest local ingredients. Every week's market offers something new. It's the start of peak tourist season in Santa Fe, and locals and visitors alike flock to the Santa Fe Railyard district, where the market is filled with a local variety of artisanal foods, fresh produce, plants and flowers—and, of course, art! The farmers' market pavilion at the Railyard offers a range of festivals and markets throughout the year, like the popular Green Chile Cheeseburger Smackdown and local craft brew festivals, along with the regular market schedules. The Railyard has become one of the cultural centers of this small city where everyone is welcome.

The water tower at the Santa Fe Railyard is a beacon of community and celebration.

The market started off with a small group of farmers who would sell produce out of the back of their trucks in the late 1960s. During the early 1970s, the League of Women Voters, along with the County Extension Office, organized to have the market relocated to the parking lot of St. Anne's Church. From there, the market moved around from Alto Street to Sanbusco and then finally to the Railyard. It took many years and a lot of community support and donations, but the farmers' market is thriving in its permanent home. Over the past decade, the Santa Fe Farmers' Market has been recognized by various publications as one of the top farmers' markets in the country and is one of over sixty markets in New Mexico. The Santa Fe Farmers' Market has always had the policy of allowing only local vendors. Today, it has over 136 members, 80 percent of whom sell minimally processed foods (meats, dairy, eggs, produce) and 20 percent selling local crafts and goods (i.e. baked goods, herbal products from local herbs, etc.). Keeping it local gives customers the ability to connect with their broader community while putting their dollars back into the local economy.

Ernestina Martinez, at the Santa Fe Farmers' Market, stands by one of her red chile ristras, which she made with the chiles she farms in Chimayó.

Ernestina Martinez is an example of one of the many farmers at the market. She continued farming chile on her father's land in Chimayó after he passed away in 1987. She grows about three acres of chile and a couple more of other produce. Her land race chile has been passed down from generation to generation. As she continues to farm, some of her children and grandchildren, along with her brother, help out, and she hopes her son will continue the chile farming tradition. She sells fresh chile, decorative ristras and red chile powder. She is one of half a dozen farmers who still grow chile in Chimayó and have enough to sell at the markets rather than just growing enough for their own use. "The flavor of Chimayó chile is the best chile in New Mexico. We eat it year round," she says, adding, "We've had a really good year this year. We've had a lot of rain, so it's been good." If you can't catch Ernestina at her booth, you can take a short trip up to Chimayó, where she sells on the side of State Road 76 #644 during chile season.

THE FUTURE OF CHILE IN NEW MEXICO

People use statistics and numbers to get a summary of where we stand on a particular issue. For the chile pepper industry in New Mexico, the statistics paint an unfortunate picture of the current status of farming New Mexican chile. It's important to remember when reviewing statistics that they don't prove a definitive truth; rather, they offer a rough outline. Nevertheless, the outline for the overall picture is alarming. Hopefully by pointing out the facts as a community, we can find more solutions to ensure the future of our chile industry.

New Mexico Chile Statistics

As of 2004, 60 percent of chiles in the United States were grown in New Mexico. Worth more than $250 million, the chile industry annually contributes over $400 million to the local economy and provides five thousand full-time and over ten thousand part-time jobs. With more than 70 percent of the crop originating in the southern part of the state—namely, Doña Ana, Hidalgo and Luna Counties—it is the third-largest cash crop of New Mexico, and that's why its rapid and recent decline is so alarming. Since the early 1990s, New Mexico has seen over 75 percent of its harvested chile acreage, and half of the amount planted, disappear. The efforts of the New Mexico Department of Agriculture are meaningful, but unfortunately the organic outfit accounts for only 1 to 2 percent of the state's overall acreage.

This is a trend that begs year-to-year comparison. Between 2012 and 2013, the harvested acreage dropped another 16 percent. That same year, the value as sold from the field fell more than 30 percent, from $65.4 million to $49.8 million. The decline slowed slightly in 2014, falling by just over 25 percent. Lest there be hope that the market did not shrink along with the acreage, the 2014 overall yield of 58,700 tons was down by more than 10 percent from 2013. For a crop that is loved by its state and the country at large—green chile sauce was voted America's most iconic food by *USA Today*—it is in dire straits. Though New Mexico dominates the domestic chile market, 82 percent of chiles consumed in the United States is imported. The largest exporter is China, producing nearly half of all the chiles consumed in the world.

43

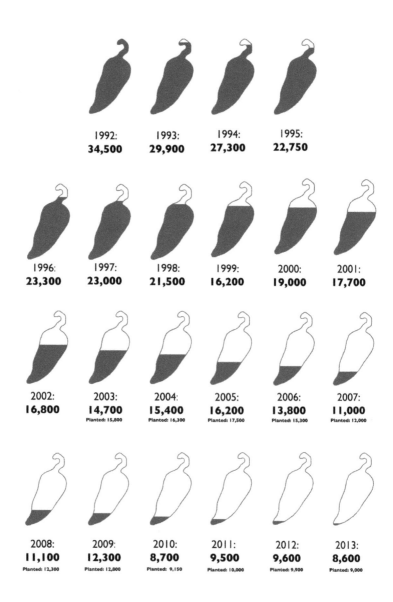

1992: **34,500** 1993: **29,900** 1994: **27,300** 1995: **22,750**

1996: **23,300** 1997: **23,000** 1998: **21,500** 1999: **16,200** 2000: **19,000** 2001: **17,700**

2002: **16,800** 2003: **14,700** Planted: 15,800 2004: **15,400** Planted: 16,300 2005: **16,200** Planted: 17,500 2006: **13,800** Planted: 15,300 2007: **11,000** Planted: 12,000

2008: **11,100** Planted: 12,300 2009: **12,300** Planted: 12,800 2010: **8,700** Planted: 9,150 2011: **9,500** Planted: 10,000 2012: **9,600** Planted: 9,900 2013: **8,600** Planted: 9,000

DECREASE IN ACRES HARVESTED OF CHILIE

The shocking 75 percent decline of chile peppers harvested in New Mexico over the past twenty years.

With a labor force stretched thin financially and in numbers, the current trends of the chile industry could have serious consequences on the workforce and economy of the state. More than twenty-one million American workers (15 percent of the total U.S. workforce) produce, process and sell the nation's food. Of every dollar earned by farmers and ranchers in the United States, only sixteen cents goes into their pocket, with the rest going to wages and materials for production, processing, marketing, transportation and distribution. America's farmers are few (less than 2 percent of the country is directly involved in agricultural production) and aging (with just 6 percent under thirty-five and an average age of fifty-eight).

Contributing Factors to the Decline of Chile Grown

CLIMATE AND DROUGHT

According to the National Oceanic and Atmospheric Administration (NOAA), 73 percent of New Mexico is in moderate to severe drought. Reservoir storage is below capacity at nearly all lakes across the state; average statewide reservoir storage is at only 24 percent capacity. Farmers in the southern part of New Mexico have resorted to installing expensive drip systems or using well water since adequate irrigation from Elephant Butte is not possible throughout the season. Several farmers who have wells have found that there is too much salt content in the water to safely water their crops. The increased salinity is an indicator that the ground water supply is running out. Radical change in climate—such as severe hail and rainstorms—can destroy crops overnight. Early or late freezes can also wipe out crops if planted too early or too late. These are factors that farmers have had to deal with for millennia, but unlike before, there is more of a challenge today to predict weather patterns. Risks are always taken, oftentimes costing the farmer.

LABOR

Chile farmers depend on migrant workers to pick green chiles by hand. The cost of hiring labor in the United States is much higher than in Mexico or other countries that don't have such strict labor laws. Although migrant workers make on average less than minimum wage, the farmers are caught in a difficult crossroads trying to compete with chiles coming into the United States at a much lower cost.

Chile pickers quickly work to pick the red chiles after a frost in Hatch. *Courtesy of Hatch Chile Store.*

PESTS AND DISEASES

Throughout much of New Mexico, chile diseases, pests and climate factors are the most costly to farmers. The curly top virus is the most notorious and destructive, attacking the plants' leaves and roots. Several other pests and viruses prove to be just as costly, like alfalfa mosaic virus, bacterial leaf spot, blossom end rot, cucumber mosaic virus, pepper mottle virus, phytophthora, root rot, root-knot nematode and pepper weevil. Many of these are due to climate factors, naturally weakening the plants. Having too much water in the soil can lead to phytophthora, or "chile wilt." This disease led the majority of crops in Hatch dying when a large rainstorm came through and the valley flooded in 2006. While scientists at the Chile Pepper Institute continue to work on breeding peppers that are more tolerant, it's often the case that the only solution for a farmer to save his crop (and his livelihood) is to spare no expense and spray the crop with some form of pesticide, herbicide or fungicide. These sprays add to the overall cost of the crop, which ultimately could still be lost if other factors contribute to its decline.

LIFESTYLE

Throughout American society, we have become disenchanted with the notion of farming or becoming a rancher or farmer. As young adults go to college, fewer are returning to farm life or choosing agriculture as a career path. Overall, adults over the age of fifty grow the majority of chile in New Mexico. In the northern farming communities, where there are fewer farms, there are even fewer young people taking on the business. With the decrease in younger people wanting to farm—especially chile, a crop that needs a lot of attention and care—many family farms are deciding to to shut down and sell the property.

What Does This Mean for Chile in New Mexico?

The facts, numbers and statistics point downward. Should we feel helpless about where we are as a state and country, especially regarding a crop that is so dear to our hearts? No, we shouldn't. We need to become more aware of the situation so that, as a community, as a state, we can make informed decisions and act on them. Labeling programs and laws aren't the only solution. The way I see it, we already have national attention and admiration for New Mexican chile and cuisine, but few people want to be part of the hard work that gets chiles on our plates. I have heard several times that there aren't enough

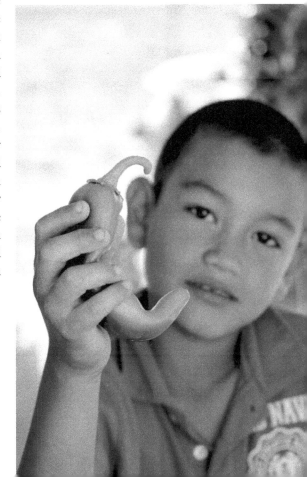

A young chile fan holds up a prized green chile that his family farmed and sold at the Hatch Chile Festival.

Left: Students learn to pollinate and check for diseases among many other skills encouraged through the NMSU breeding program. *Courtesy of the Chile Pepper Institute.*

Below: NMSU's Chile Pepper Institute Teaching Garden allows students, locals and visitors to learn about the myriad chile varieties and home cultivation. *Courtesy of the Chile Pepper Institute.*

chiles grown in New Mexico to support the demand by restaurants. Part of this is due to the lack of natural resources, like water, to which farmers have access. Many farmers I have met would prefer to farm more chiles but are unable to do so due to increasing costs and lack of water. I do believe that there will always be chiles grown in New Mexico—most likely, people growing their desired varieties in their backyards because what's grown commercially and available at the grocery stores are chiles from Mexico, China or Spain. While the social, economic and climatic factors are all connected to the decline of chile growth, there are choices each individual can make that will contribute to supporting our chile culture. Here are some suggestions:

We need to start getting children acquainted with farming practices at a young age and introducing them to the joy of growing food. By breaking the social stigma that farming isn't a desired career or that it doesn't lead to success, we can encourage young people to aspire to this type of work. We can instruct and inform them on how to be successful farmers and introduce them to people who already are. We should pay attention to farmers like Matt Romero, who invite and educate young people about farming practices. Hopefully more New Mexican universities will offer school credit to students who want to learn how to work on farms. The Chile Pepper Institute has done a great job working with children, students and adults, showing them how to work with chile peppers and the type of environments they adapt to best. These programs and institutions should be recognized for their achievements, as well as supported financially.

Chris Franzoy, a great-grandson of Joseph Franzoy, who also happens to be Faron Lytle's cousin, is a fourth-generation farmer in Hatch. He is the owner of Young Guns Produce. Young Guns distributes chiles to over thirty-six different states, and Chris is proud to continue his great-grandfather's legacy of growing and distributing chiles around the world. The Franzoy family originated from Italy, and they were partially responsible for homesteading and turning the Hatch Valley into a farming community. Chris talks about how "we feel responsible for carrying on the family tradition." To him, fresh Hatch chile is a delicacy because it's available for only about two months during the year. Chris spoke about being unsure during his college years if he wanted to pursue farming because he felt there were so many foreign competitors that have much lower costs, and that makes them difficult to compete with. However, Chris chose to come back and farm, to continue to promote his family's chile legacy and offer

Young Guns' green chiles, freshly harvested from Hatch fields, are placed in barrels to be cleaned and shipped out in boxes throughout the country.

consumers a quality product. "Hatch chile is one of the best things that has ever happened to New Mexico," he says. "The chile we grow here is a unique commodity, unlike anywhere else in the world."

New Mexicans and fans of our chile can help by putting their money where it matters—by purchasing chiles directly from New Mexican farmers at local farmers' markets or at roadside stands. These types of transactions put money directly back to the source and acknowledge their service. Buying any type of food this way cuts out several additional fees—like transportation or processing—that fall mostly on the farmer. Obviously, not everyone can do this, especially if you live outside New Mexico. Ask chile vendors where their chile comes from. If they say Hatch, ask them what *colonia*. Ask what varieties they offer and see if any match the New Mexican chile varieties listed in this book. Ask New Mexican and even non–New Mexican restaurants, cafés, food trucks and diners if their chiles come from New Mexico.

We understand the popularity of chiles worldwide. It makes sense that people want to grow New Mexican varieties of chile peppers in their home

Local staples like Chile Toreado are popular lunch destinations to get a "chile fix."

states, but hopefully they don't sell them as "Hatch chiles." For those who choose to go the distance to buy their chile products from New Mexico, they are contributing to a four-hundred-year-old history and culture and building up the economy around this significant crop.

Part III

FARMING

THE FUN OF FARMING WITH MATT ROMERO

"Don't panic! It's organic, and we're Hispanic!" Matt Romero calls out as he rotates his metal chile roaster, blasting waves of savory capsicum chile smells into the crowd of onlookers and farmers' market shoppers. "Free smells!" He captivates them all first with the smell of his farm's organic roasted chiles and then with his wit and charismatic personality.

If it is your first time going to the Santa Fe Farmers' Market, I can guarantee that vendor Matt Romero will make a lasting impression. He is typically out in the front of his booth wearing his pink farmers' market apron and sautéing his myriad potatoes or handing out slices of his carrots. He's the life of the market, and everyone knows it. Loyal patrons eagerly discuss the variety of flavor in his produce and what new recipes he recommends. If Matt weren't a farmer, he certainly would be a foodie and an enthusiastic supporter of organic farming practices.

Matt has been growing chile for over two decades and has developed a reputation throughout northern New Mexico (especially Santa Fe) as the go-to guy for fresh, organic produce. Local chefs eager to buy directly from him fight over his fresh-off-the-field produce to incorporate into seasonal menus. He farms chile with a keen insight into the chef's needs. He spent over two decades in the restaurant industry working under world-class chefs and learning their techniques. When Matt and his wife were offered the opportunity to care for a small orchard in Velarde, he became enthralled

Matt Romero jokes with his customers as he roasts his "Alcalde Improved" variety of chile at the Santa Fe Farmers' Market.

and jumped at the opportunity to learn more about farming from friends and family. His farm is located in Alcalde, just north of Santa Fe, and he is proud to continue his family's traditions of farming—but especially of farming chile. The opportunity Matt was given to learn to farm and take care of a piece of property is something he has never forgotten. He has become a farming educator to younger generations that are also interested in learning sustainable farming practices. Matt invites young students and non-students to his farm, where he instructs them on how to start a farm and make money doing it.

Matt grows a variation of the "Española Improved" variety discussed in more detail in the "History of Chile" section. Little do most people know, but this variety was grown and tested at the NMSU sustainable agricultural science center in Alcalde, just down the road from Matt's farm. Alcalde is up the Rio Grande, about nine miles north of Española. This distance might not be significant to most, but as mentioned previously, the slightest difference in soil, altitude and climate all have an effect on crops grown. Those nine miles—which is the same distance between Chimayó and Española—translate into a different kind of pepper. Most people with discerning palates would agree that there is a difference of flavor between the dried red chile pods of Chimayó and those of Española. Chimayó chiles tend to have more of an earthy sweetness, while Española chiles have a high heat that finishes with a natural smokiness. The same notion applies to the green chile pods from Española and Alcalde. Alcalde and Española chiles are very similar; however, Alcalde chiles tend to have a higher heat level.

Matt farms what he calls "Alcalde Improved," a Romero family–grown variety. It is a descendent of the "Española Improved" developed by Nakayama and Matta in the mid-1970s about a quarter mile away from Matt's farm. This variety has the traditional flavor and heat with a larger, thicker pod than the traditional land race variety, or what most people at the time would call the "local variety." Matt's uncle, Arthur Martinez, was given some of the first seeds of "Española Improved" before its release over thirty years ago. Matt's uncle was a knowledgeable horticulturalist and every season selected pods for confirmation based on the quality of pod, plant, flavor and yield. He would save the best of each season and pick the rest. Doing this over time helped develop the chile every year so that it adapted to the specific climate and soil of his farm in Alcalde. It adapted so well that a couple of years ago, a frost came through after the chiles had already grown to almost three inches in length. During the frost, temperatures dropped below twenty-eight degrees Fahrenheit, and Matt lost 80 percent of his crop of eggplants but didn't lose a single "Alcalde Improved" chile pepper. "I don't know if it's because the plants have become frost tolerant or because they were low to the ground, but consistently after a frost, we haven't lost a single chile pepper." Matt adds, "Remember, this chile has never been to Española; it's only ever been through Española."

Matt quickly realized that not everyone likes the heat of the "Alcalde Improved," so he got some "Joe Parker" seed from NMSU. Bosland developed this variety in the 1990s, and it was bred for people who like a nice mild heat. The variety is uniform in size, roasts and peels easily but doesn't have as much heat. "This is the chile I raised my kids on, and they trust me now," he jokes. "If people are asking for a mild chile, it better be mild, and this is the pepper for those folks." What most people aren't aware of is that all peppers, except for a couple of bell pepper varieties, will mature to a red color. Peppers that start life purple, green or even yellow will turn red upon full maturity. Matt notes:

As peppers turn red, they become less bitter; they become sweet, and they develop a brix, which is a sugar content. Red peppers, as we know, have a short shelf life; they lose their firmness, which is why they can't be

Matt Romero's chile field in Alcalde is harvested to sell at market. *Photo by Paige Davidson.*

transported to other cities around the country. We pick them today, roast and sell them the next day at the farmers' market in Santa Fe when they still have that natural sweetness, that full flavor...I bet we're the only city that does something like that. That is definitely something you could never buy at any store.

Some distributors will sell chiles that were picked when they had stripes of red on the peppers and then ripen them in ethylene gas rooms. Produce naturally emits ethylene gas as it ripens; the same method has been used for decades with bananas. This ripening method creates a pepper that is fully red in color but that hasn't developed the sugar content of a naturally ripened pepper. Many fruits and vegetables are ripened in alternative ways so that when people shop at a supermarket, they can buy produce that has the desired texture and ripeness but often lacks the depth of flavor. As farm-to-table movements grow throughout the country, one of the many examples they give to consumers is the difference in taste between a product that was ripened naturally on the vine and one ripened using an alternative method. Matt articulates this very well to his returning customers every week at the market: "Taste the difference and you'll return. Only nature can produce this kind of flavor." Both his popularity and his sales at the market prove it.

Through Matt's education and learned practices from his family members, he understands the challenge when farming organic produce and the details that go into caring for his crops. For his direct-seeded crops of chile, he waits three years before planting chile in the same soil. Rotating his crops (as well as planting cover crops) allows the soil to maintain its natural nutrients and to prevent diseases in the plants. In Matt's experience, applying compost early in the season, moderating the soil moisture and making sure the highs and lows stay within range all help keep his plants healthy and free of disease. According to Matt, today there are only about a handful of people left in the Alcalde Valley who farm chile for their livelihood. "It's a dying art," he says. Most people fifty years ago in northern New Mexico lived off food grown on their own land. Back then, most people couldn't afford to have refrigerators or ice boxes to preserve their food, so they grew food that would store well—like chile.

I love farming chile for the smile I see on people's faces—that's the payback right there. People saying "thank you for growing this"…that means a lot to me to see people legitimately thankful for what I do. My family never farmed to make any money; they only ever farmed to eat. I left for twenty-

Matt Romero stands in his organic chile field located in Alcalde. *Photo by Paige Davidson.*

three years, and when I returned, I thought the valley had changed. But it hadn't, I had changed. When you leave the farm and you go off in the world and you see some of the finer things in life, you realize that the best food in the world is the food grown in your own backyard, not what you buy in the store.

When you develop a relationship with local farmers, you get to see what they are all about; you can see the way they care for their food and how it satisfies the people they sustain. They are not hiding behind a label or an image of a bright sunny day with perfectly colored fields and larger-than-life produce growing in it. Compost does not smell pretty, bugs and spiders living on plants aren't inviting, muddy soil and flying dirt aren't glamorous, but these are the characteristics of a real farm. The unglamorous and dirty business of growing food has not fundamentally changed over the millennia, no matter what technology we develop. The common thread of knowing farmers are that they are honest about what they grow and deeply proud to provide it to the public, especially an item that is rooted in the culture. Removing the social interest of being connected to the land is not what makes chile or any food taste better. The beauty of food, of chile, is all that sweat and dirtiness is necessary to provide a rich, complex and bold spice that we eat every day all year long.

BERRIDGE FAMILY FARMS: A CHILE DAY

The first beams of morning light spread across the Hatch Valley, slowly reaching out as they begin to caress the top branches of the pecan orchards. Little by little, the sunrays reach the chile plants, many of which have already matured to red. Cool morning dew briefly sits on the leaves, but the plants quickly drink up and exhale, ready for the sunny day. Dust clouds form as several cars make their way down the dirt road toward a large shed. Excitement lingers in the wake of the fallen dust.

For my family, Berridge Family Chile Day is as big as Christmas Eve. Family members both young and old gather in Hatch at my cousins' farm to turn fresh red chiles into red chile sauce. Because fresh red chile is ripe for only a brief period and has a short shelf life, making fresh red chile sauce (as opposed to rehydrating dried chiles) requires that the sauce be made within a day or two of when the red chile pods are picked. This tight timing, combined with the volume of labor required, means that most people in New Mexico get the majority of their red chile sauce from dried chile pods that were set out to dry in the sun, hung on ristras or turned into powder. While the taste difference may be subtle or indistinguishable to a non-local, a real New Mexican will know and appreciate it.

Every two years, my family gathers for this one day so that we can take home gallons of fresh red chile and freeze it to last the next two years. Our red chile sauce production process is unique to our family and has evolved over generations to maximize productivity. It should be mentioned that within each step, there are positions of seniority. I've never been in charge of making rue and adding the seasoning because I haven't done it enough. I usually stick with hanging out on the chopping line, appreciating the beauty of each chile.

Step one in the process: picking the fresh red chiles off the vine just as they have turned fully red and before they've lost too much thickness or size. Deciding on the weekend to make the sauce changes every year, as it is always weather dependent. Some years, the chile plants sprout later due to a cold spring, while in other years the pods start to mature early. Once the pods are picked, family members make the pilgrimage to Hatch from their homes all over the Southwest. Everyone starts to work at the crack of dawn, and we don't stop until lunchtime.

Berridge family members on the chopping line remove stems and seeds from the cleaned red chile pods before they are boiled.

Boiling down freshly picked red chile is one step of the process to make fresh red chile sauce performed by the Berridge family at biannual gatherings in Hatch.

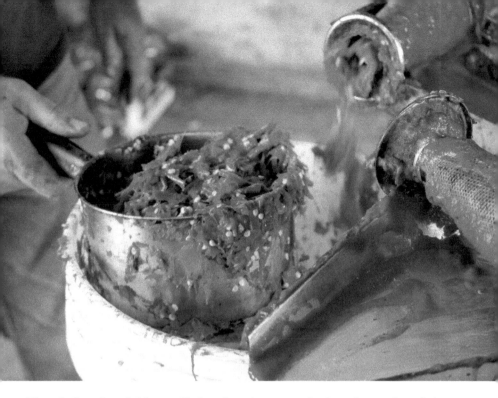

The pulp from the red chile gets sifted out from the sauce so that it can be sent through the purée process again.

Step two: after the fresh pods are picked, they are washed and scrubbed clean. Then a team works on chopping off the stems and removing the seeds. Meanwhile, preparation of the other chile stations begins. Large caldrons are filled with water and heated to a boil over a propane-fueled flame.

Step three: the cleaned pods are added to the boiling water and steeped until the water starts to turn a slight yellowish red color, at which point the chile pods are ready to be taken out. The once firm chile pods are now the texture of a cooked lasagna noodle.

Step four: the pods are sifted out from any remaining water and put into a type of grinding machine called a squeegee. Most of the men in our family prefer to work this step, as it involves power tools and machinery. The hydrated and steaming hot chiles then enter the grinder, which sifts out any large chunks of skin and pulp. The skins and pulp are sent through a couple more times to extract as much chile meat as possible. Everyone in this process ends the day with chile on their shirts, pants and faces and generally looks like they've had an encounter on a battlefield. The resulting purée of steaming hot red chile sauce is collected in a ten-gallon bucket to be sent to the next station.

Elaine Mitchell is ready to pour her chile into containers to freeze for the year.

Step five: the large buckets are taken to the cooking area, where most of my aunts and cousins have large stewpots prepared with a simple roux consisting of oil, flour and garlic. Once the red chile is poured in each pot, it is seasoned for each particular family's taste preferences. My aunt and uncle prefer their red chile just with a little salt and garlic and that's it. Other family members prefer their chile with a little salt, garlic, cumin and oregano. Once the chile has reached the desired taste, it is sent to get packaged.

Step six: each family is responsible for bringing their own bottles, jars and Tupperware to store the chile they plan to take home. Most families take extra containers for their extended family and close friends who live too far to make the journey to Hatch. Once the chile is poured into containers, it's labeled for the particular family member or family group. When it is finished cooking, the chile sauce needs to sit out and cool off. Once all the containers have been filled, along with a couple extra (just in case), chile day is complete. The red chile sauce, if put in a large glass gallon jar, will need to be transferred to an ice chest to cool off and stay fresh for the drive home.

Step seven: a little before noon, my cousin Lance starts to set up his portable grills, each in the shape of a large disc. He oils the bottom of the discs and cooks seasoned ground beef. Family members assist him in making large red chile enchiladas for all sixty to eighty family members present. A coat of the fresh red chile we just made gets ladled out and then topped with a full layer of corn tortillas, to be followed by another layer of red chile before the seasoned ground beef, which is sprinkled with onions and cheese and topped with another layer of chile. This procedure continues on until there are about six layers. Next, my cousin

Bobby starts to cook some eggs over-easy for those who want to add an egg to top off the enchilada. About ten minutes later, the entire property starts to get real quiet except for the sounds of a few "hmmms" and "s' goods." The rule typically goes: if you don't work, then you don't get fed, and no one wants to miss out on enchiladas that taste like manna from the heavens.

Step eight: once everyone is home, the sauce is transferred from the large jars into small plastic Tupperware, eliminating as much air as possible since leaving air in a container could lead to bacteria entering if not frozen properly. For most New Mexicans and for many of my family members, there is always a separate freezer for chile. We pack it away like the chile apocalypse has come because nothing would be worse for a New Mexican than to run out of chile. It happened once to my parents, and it wasn't pretty. My inner she-hulk might come out and charge down the street, demolishing any chile ristras in sight (and I'm only half kidding).

My favorite part of coming together with my extended family members for one day has been different throughout my life. Some of my earliest, very faint memories are of feeling cotton on the plants for the first time or pulling an onion out of the ground. I was thrilled to have time to play with my many cousins as we chased one another around the pecan orchards as the giant trees looked down on our delight. We would start "pecan wars," chucking pecans at one another, dodging the hits and making tactical team maneuvers. Sure, we would get some kind of work done, but mostly we just played in the fields, expanding our imaginations. As I started to get older, chile day meant spending time with some of my older family members whom I see only occasionally and listening to their stories of growing up on the farm. Learning about the past and our family's history has given each one of us a unique perspective on what future we want both independently and as a family. The work never felt like work because there was always so much laughter and teasing getting to know my extensive family and all its many generations. Chile for us, just like for many New Mexican families, is more than a traditional food; it's what brings families and friends together and builds memories for a lifetime—memories we will share with our children so they, too, might understand where they have come from and share in the pride and responsibility of what we do.

FROM RISTRAS TO RELLENOS WITH SICHLER FAMILY FARMS

In the fall, driving around Albuquerque with the windows down is about getting a cool breeze circulating through the car while smelling the roasting of green chiles throughout the city. One of the most recognized locations in Albuquerque is on San Mateo Boulevard at the Sichler Farms fruit stand. The Sichlers emigrated from Germany to the middle of the Rio Grande Valley, near Los Lunas, in 1868. They started off farming Brussels sprouts, broccoli and cabbage and soon discovered that these vegetables didn't go over so well with the local community. People at the time didn't really know how to cook with these foods, but they knew chile. So the Sichlers switched to growing chile and have continued doing so for over six generations in New Mexico.

John Sichler and his wife, Eleanor, are one branch of the New Mexican Sichlers that farm chile. When John proposed to Eleanor over thirty years ago, he asked, "Will you marry me…and can we open a fruit stand?" Today, with the help of their children Tim and Naomi, their fruit stand has been in business for over twenty-eight years, selling a variety of chile and non-chile products from August to October. Eleanor decided that they needed to sell pumpkins of all sizes in October, and in recent years, the sight of red chiles and pumpkins has become part of the New Mexican fall aesthetic that attracts people from all around town. The stand also displays an assortment of ristras that John and Eleanor have hung, bringing color and vibrancy to the city of Albuquerque. I chuckle at the small, four-inch ristras hanging alongside the enormous red chile ristras of seven feet tall.

"Climate, culture and the people are perfectly designed for chile," John says. "You can go anywhere at any time, especially during the fall when it's roasting, and hear people talking about chile." John's concerns about farming chile are similar to those of the farmers I have met in the northern New Mexico communities. Chile is getting harder and more expensive to grow, which is confirmed by the official statistics. There has been a 75 percent decrease in the amount of chiles harvested over the past twenty years, which is an enormous decline in a short amount of time for such a historically loved crop. John notes:

> *It's becoming more difficult. We go through intense drought periods, and we're growing in population. Water is a very scarce resource, and then there's the labor situation. It's becoming so hard to make a living doing*

The fruit stand of Sichler Farms in Albuquerque is part of the New Mexican experience, with beautiful colors and the uplifting smell of roasted chiles filling the air in the summer and fall.

Father and son John and Tim Sichler stand in front of their massive chile ristras, which they sell at their Sichler family fruit stand off San Mateo Boulevard in Albuquerque.

this. You have to do this and something else for most farmers. People will always grow some chile, but in order to grow it, there will continue to be price increases as the cost to grow the crop continues to increase. Only time will tell if we can continue to keep doing this for a price people can afford.

Right now, many chile farmers depend on loyal customers buying directly from where they roast or paying for chile to be shipped frozen to their doors if they happen to be out-of-state clients. John observed from his own business, "People not from here schedule annual trips around getting their chile from New Mexico. I would say all chile farmers depend on that kind of customer." After a sigh, the subject moves to our favorite chile dishes. John says, "If I had to have a last meal for some reason, it would be a Frito Pie in a bowl with new crop pinto beans, red chile, fried hamburger meat, fresh tomatoes, diced onions and topped with cheddar cheese." He licks his lips. "Although I have a favorite chile sandwich—it's the best!"

Part IV

THE RESTAURANTS

THE SHED RESTAURANT: A LIVING HISTORY

Over four hundred years old, Santa Fe is deeply rooted in history, and many of the local restaurants have embraced this history as part of their ambiance. There's a feeling one gets from dining in a place that is filled with expansive history—a feeling as if the secrets of time buried deep within the walls will reach out and whisper their excitement to still be seen and touched, to still be part of history. The Shed in Santa Fe is one of these places. On a warm summer day, one block from the historic plaza on East Palace Street, in a small courtyard called Prince Patio filled with blossoming roses, trumpet vines and hollyhocks, the aroma of garlic, chile, blue corn and beans fills the air and is even more captivating than the garden. It is this smell that invites you into the remodeled 1692 hacienda. The Shed started with a creative couple with a taste for cuisines of the world and a strong work ethic.

Polly and Thornton Carswell moved from Illinois to Carmel, California, and then finally came to Santa Fe in 1950. Polly was always interested in art and different types of cooking, learning from family and neighbors as they moved around. The couple would sell soups and sandwiches at Hyde Park just outside Santa Fe to skiers as they came down from the mountain. The Carswells' food was well received, and they were asked to run a small restaurant for a couple of seasons, serving skiers at what was called the Sierra Lodge on the ski mountain. Polly's

Artwork by Gisella Loeffer outside the Shed restaurant is a symbol of home for many New Mexicans.

knack for creativity and love of food led the couple to open a small restaurant on Burro Alley in 1953. The Shed was just that—a shed on Burro Alley that was once a place where people would come to unload their supplies and wood and put up their donkeys before heading to a bar or eatery. This location was more or less a burro parking lot for locals and travelers. By the 1950s, the use of burros in town had long gone, so Polly and Thornton, along with their neighbors, worked on renovating and converting the old donkey shed into a twenty-two-seat lunch and dinner restaurant. To locals who have known the Shed their whole lives, it might come as a surprise that some of the first dishes served weren't chile dishes but rather beef stroganoff, chicken cacciatore and even lobster tail.

The Lensic, the Alley Theatre and the El Paseo Theatre were all within close walking distance to the Shed, and people came to enjoy a home cooked–type meal before or after a show. Word spread, and the couple was doing a good turn of business. Polly, having a creative mind, learned recipes from her neighbors, and Thornton helped execute the meals on a larger scale, making sure the taste and quality were always consistent. Less than a decade later, in 1960, the couple sold the property on Burro Alley and moved to their current location off Lincoln Avenue, just one block from Santa Fe's historic plaza. Although the location was close to the Santa Fe Plaza, it took people some time to seek it out. The days of serving only twenty-two people at a time were long gone, and the restaurant became immensely popular.

Courtney Carswell, Polly and Thornton's son, credits a couple of families in town for introducing the Carswells to New Mexican–style cuisine:

> *We lived in a neighborhood called Banana Hill, and several neighbors introduced us to the traditional northern New Mexican style of cooking. I remember Yolanda Vigil served me red chile and pinto beans. It was my first time experiencing such simple but delicious food. The Carrillos were also neighbors, and incidentally, their daughter Consuelo started working as a cook for my parents when she was in high school and stayed with the family for over forty years. At their house, they would always have a bowl of green chile on the table. Chile was just what everyone ate.*

During the 1960s, the demand for New Mexican cuisine in Santa Fe was so high that the menu had almost completely changed, though it kept some signature non–New Mexican dishes from before, like the French garlic bread that pairs nicely with any chile dish. Courtney's parents ran the restaurant from 1953 to 1970, and their appreciation for food rubbed off on him. Little by little, they started to withdraw as he became more involved in the operation. When Courtney took over, the Shed hadn't had green chile as an option for over forty-five years. Green chile comes at a higher cost and has a short season of fresh availability, which makes it a more difficult item to maintain. However, as time passed, Courtney recognized that green chile was just as popular with his customers. The family has gone to great lengths to ensure that their customers are receiving the same quality food time and time again. Finding a green chile provider would be no different.

The Carwells became connoisseurs of chile peppers, choosing the Sandia variety to make their red and green chile sauces from a particular Franzoy family member's farm in Hatch. The Carswells have been purchasing their chiles for over twenty-five years from the farm in Hatch to make their popular sauces. In 2003, the Shed won the James Beard Foundation Award, supporting what locals knew for decades to be true: the Shed makes quality food that is true to traditional styles of New Mexican

cuisine. Courtney's children, Sarah and Josh, joined the family business in the late 1990s, helping to evolve the Shed and its sister restaurant, La Choza (Spanish for "the Shed"). Today, the Shed bottles its red chile sauce and dried chile products for customers who have moved away from New Mexico or for those who just have a hankering for the product to buy and take home.

Courtney reflected on what his family's restaurant means to the community, describing it as an extension of his own family: "This is an extension of our home, and we love being able to see families come here for lunch or celebrations and watch their families grow and evolve and newer generations continuing to make the Shed or La Choza a

Left, top: An enchilada and taco plate from the Shed.

Left, bottom: *La Choza* is Spanish for "the Shed," and it is the sister restaurant to the Shed. Both have been owned and operated by the Carswell family for three generations.

Opposite: An authentic New Mexican dish, which the locals call "#4 with an egg." It is otherwise known as a blue corn–layered enchilada smothered with red chile, topped with an egg over-easy and served with a side of pinto beans and posole.

part of their traditions. People say they come here first after landing at the airport before even going home to get their "chile fix," and our food is what reminds them that they're home. We have a connection to our community through our food."

People have been returning for the Shed's unchanged recipes for over fifty years. For Sarah and Josh, it took leaving home for many years to realize the importance chile had on their lives and their personal identities. They came to the realization that what they provide, and the culture they are part of, is unique—and that it's worth preserving and continuing. Sarah explains, "We tell our staff that this is more than a restaurant; it is a part of living history. They see when a fourth- or fifth-generation Shed eater comes in and says, 'This is where my grandparents ate every weekend or my great-grandparents,' feeling a part of the fabric of our community that has great meaning." The color of the walls might change and the chairs might be upgraded, but people return to the Shed or La Choza for a bite that tastes like home, to eat at a place filled with the memories of celebrating a graduation, a birthday, an engagement or the simple nostalgia of cooking enchiladas in grandma's kitchen.

BEST. BREAKFAST. EVER.

The smell of delicious, crunchy bacon and fresh-brewed coffee wafts through the air as I near Tia Sophia's Restaurant for a traditional Christmas-style breakfast burrito. Comfy dark wooden booths line a restaurant adorned with Pueblo-style rugs, mariachi hats, colorful fiesta dresses and, of course, ristras. Two burritos smothered in red chile get delivered to a nearby table, and half the guests waiting to receive their breakfasts stare at the couple like dogs waiting for a scrap to fly in their direction. Mouths salivate as onlookers silently share in the first bite of the burritos. Tia Sophia's is a local favorite, close to the historic plaza in Santa Fe and boasting the liveliness of downtown without the couture price tag.

The history of the breakfast and lunch restaurant starts with Toni and Sophia, an immigrant couple from Greece who settled in the Atrisco barrio of Albuquerque. Being a Greek family, they opened up a restaurant that, like many others, served recipes borrowed from their neighbors. Two of the couple's children, Jim and Georgia, would go on to open their own restaurants years later.

Jim Maryol finished his degree after he came back from the Vietnam War and became an insurance adjuster in Colorado Springs. Jim and his wife, Ann, wanted to move to New Mexico. When he spoke with his sister Georgia, who had recently opened a restaurant, she suggested they move to Santa Fe and open one as well. Jim's cousin Ignacio suggested they name the restaurant after his aunt Sophia (Jim's mother), calling it "Tia Sophia" (which means Aunt Sophia). Jim and Ann thought the name sounded great and opened the restaurant in 1975, moving its location closer to Santa Fe's historic plaza in 1982. The couple's son, Nick, left the finance world and bought the business from his parents, effective January 1, 2015. Nick credits Connie and Jenny Aargon, who worked in their kitchen for many years, for giving the restaurant's dishes their signature flavor. Although Nick has taken on the family business, there are few things he has changed or wants to change.

"I let the kitchen run itself," he says. "They're pros. I updated the payroll so it's done on the computer now…that's about it. I don't endeavor to change what so many people love. We want to continue to give you the best meal for the best possible price." I asked Nick if his family ever felt excluded from the culture because they weren't Hispanic. He responded, "We are a true melting pot here in New Mexico. Chile is one of the great unifiers around here. It doesn't matter if you're Hispanic, Native American or of Greek descent, chile is our soul food."

A breakfast burrito with bacon and potatoes wrapped in a flour tortilla and topped with red and green chiles and cheese from Tia Sophia's in Santa Fe.

Nick sees a profound responsibility in continuing his family's legacy of providing New Mexican meals for longtime New Mexicans, as well as for those coming to visit. The restaurant's hard workers and delicious breakfasts have been recognized on the Food Network's show *Best. Breakfast. Ever.*, featuring none other than the breakfast burrito smothered in Christmas and served with a poached egg on top. I can assure you that the reward is worth the trip if you ever have the chance to find your way into Tia Sophia's.

TASTING TRADITION AT TOMASITA'S

The red brick stationhouse built in 1904 was once the gateway for the "Chile Line," making stops throughout towns and pueblos of turn-of-the-century New Mexico, but it is now the location of Tomasita's Restaurant. The red stationhouse is a striking contrast to the plethora of adobe-style buildings and homes in Santa Fe. Just walking distance from the final Rail Runner stop at the Santa Fe Railyard, Tomasita's has become an iconic restaurant for authentic New Mexican cuisine and renowned margaritas. The entrance is

George Gundrey, owner of Atrisco Café & Bar and Tomasita's Restaurant, tends bar on a busy summer afternoon at Tomasita's in Santa Fe.

usually lined with people gathering around an appetizer of chips, guacamole and salsa or sipping on margaritas while waiting for a table (especially in the evenings). The entrance is filled with beautiful artwork leading to the main dining room lined with dark wooden booths, low-hanging antique globe light chandeliers, large ristras and dangling houseplants. The atmosphere is filled with laughter and lively conversations, especially when Mariachi Buenaventura (an all-female musical group) comes to play once a week. George Gundrey is the third-generation owner, and he also runs a sister restaurant, Atrisco Café & Bar, which is named after the neighborhood where his mother and her family grew up in Albuquerque. George's mother, Georgia Maryol, opened the original Tomasita's Restaurant on Hickox Street in 1974.

Georgia had been well acquainted with restaurant life and New Mexico food culture, coming from a Greek family that owned and operated Central Café and the Mayflower Café and growing up with northern New Mexican cuisine in the Atrisco barrio of Albuquerque. In the early 1970s, she and her son James happened upon a small café on Hickox Street and stopped in for a bite to eat. After trying a (life-changing) bean burrito smothered in red chile that reminded her of her childhood, she decided to compliment the chef.

She went into the kitchen to meet the cook and came upon Tomasita Leyba stirring a stew pot in one hand and smoking a cigarette with the other. As Georgia excitedly introduced herself and complimented her on her cooking, Tomasita nodded her head, gave a slight smile and continued on with her work. Within the following months, Georgia frequented the café as often as she could, trying everything on the menu and finding nirvana in each bite. It came to Georgia's attention that the present owner of the café was unable to continue running the business and was going to sell or close. Georgia, being unwilling to let her favorite new restaurant close, decided she would meet with the owner. The proposition was difficult for Georgia, who was unemployed, broke and raising two boys, but nevertheless, she could not resist the challenge. Georgia went to the owner and offered to assume all of his debts in exchange for the café. A couple days later, Georgia became the new owner.

With her new title of business owner, Georgia came to the café the next morning, and to her happy surprise, Tomasita was in the kitchen, already preparing and cooking for the day's customers. She gave Georgia a stern look and said, "Are you going to keep me or fire me?" With gratitude in her voice, Georgia responded, "Well, Tomasita, I think I'll just keep you." The two embarked on a friendship few encounter in a lifetime. Georgia quickly learned that the café required repair and needed new equipment and that the employees needed set business hours. She sat down with the employees and decided on set hours of operation. Georgia would work in the café from 9:00 a.m. to 9:00 p.m., employing her sons to wash and clean the dishes after school and when homework was done. With new enthusiasm oozing through the café, combined with more consistency and top-quality meals, the business started to grow, and word got out about how good Tomasita's food was. For five years, the café boomed and buzzed with loyal customers and tourists. Tomasita's extensive family became part of Georgia's family, and the two shared a profound respect for each other.

It wasn't long before Georgia, Tomasita and their team realized they had outgrown the small, thirty-two-seat café. They were ready to move to a new location when the red brick stationhouse went up for lease. The local press warned that the new location would be a disaster for the little café and it would lose its business. Georgia was concerned about losing everything they had all worked so hard for and asked Tomasita what she thought. She replied, "Tell 'em all to go to hell. Let's move!" So they did in 1979, making the Tomasita's stationhouse an American classic. Throughout the years, Tomasita's has fed several presidents, diplomats and celebrities, in

A green chile chicken blue corn burrito with a cup of red chile posole and sides of sopapilla, chips and salsa at Atrisco Café & Bar in Santa Fe.

addition to its loyal Santa Fe patrons. As Georgia has stepped back and let her cousin Ignacio (who named her brother's restaurant Tia Sophia's) and her son George take over, one thing is certain: they pay homage to Tomasita everyday. The family makes sure the kitchen is spotless, the equipment is clean and the food is top quality, using as many local and organic ingredients as possible, just as Tomasita would have done herself.

George has done his family proud by continuing the tradition at Atrisco Café, making it into a busy, classic New Mexican restaurant just as his mother had done years before. "One thing I am insanely proud of with both restaurants," George says, "is that people come in from every walk of life, every type of class, every ethnicity—they come here, and they all see someone they know."

HOLY MOLE AT CAFÉ PASQUAL'S

On any given day of the week, Café Pasqual's in Santa Fe is bustling with tourists and locals alike, usually with a line out the door. The walls are adorned with Mexican tiles and exquisite murals painted by renowned

Mexican artist Leovigildo Martinez. The ceilings are filled with bright, colorful *papel picados*; ristras hung with twinkle lights intertwined; and a large piñata-type chandelier with the finest Mexican paper flowers drawing the eye. The ambiance of this corner café will transport you to a lively town in Mexico. Once there, you will be greeted by some of the most wonderful combinations of flavors from the cuisines of Mexico and New Mexico. You might wish to start off your meal with the sweet, flavorful, mild heat of Jimmy Nardello peppers. The bright red peppers are pan fried in a little olive oil, sprinkled with a little salt and finished with a squeeze of fresh lime juice. Katharine Kagel, the chef and founder of Café Pasqual's, has devoted her life to studying, researching, preparing and serving the best-quality food for a unique experience her guests won't soon forget.

Katharine grew up in Berkeley, California, a city that embraced and celebrated ethnic foods of the world. From a young age, peppers were part of her diet, and she recalls her grandmother canning pickles with Hungarian peppers to add flavor. Her first visit to Santa Fe was in 1969, when she and a friend took a trip around the United States. The Apodaca family of Apodaca Hill took them in because they thought it uncustomary for two young girls to be traveling alone without a chaperone. "Whatever kitchen I arrived in, chile was always on the

Sweet Italian Jimmy Nardello peppers sautéed in olive oil and spritzed with lime juice join a side of dried plantains seasoned with New Mexican Chimayó red chile and salt.

Katharine Kagel's mole sauce covering organic pulled chicken, spinach and zucchini wrapped in corn tortillas with a sprinkle of cotija cheese, served with cilantro rice, jicama and oranges, is heaven on earth.

stove," Katherine says. As part of their daily routine, Katharine witnessed the tradition of eating a bowl of chile every day, and it has stuck with her ever since. She says, "Everybody is involved in the culture of chile in New Mexico; it doesn't matter if you're Native American, Hispanic, Mexican or Anglo."

Katharine moved to Santa Fe in 1978 and opened up Café Pasqual's (named after San Pasqual, the patron saint of cooks) the following year. Since the day the café opened, many types of chile have been used for its dishes. It has an entire warehouse devoted to all the chile peppers it uses—and for good reason. Some of the chiles used include Anaheims, poblanos, jalapeños, shishitos, Jimmy Nardellos, tepins, habañeros, chile de árbols, Thai chiles, cayennes, paprikas, espelettes, padróns, Chimayó dry powders, dried Anaheim green chiles, gualillos (dried mirasol), anchos (dried smoked poblano), pasillas (dried chilaca) and chipotles (dried smoked jalapeño). Katharine uses an ancient Aztec recipe to make the mole sauce for the two mole enchiladas with sides of cilantro rice, jicama and orange. The mole has twenty-four ingredients that combine different types of chile, cinnamon, banana, onions and dark bitter chocolate. From personal experience, I can assure you that many restaurants fail to make mole that has such an earthy sweet and semi-spicy mixture, and I would choose to eat Katharine's mole any day of the week. Then again, I would also eat anything on her menu. Katharine reflects on a time when "a man came in saying, 'I'm lookin' for hurtin' chile.'" She gave him an inquisitive look and said, "Well, we do flavor not pain."

In addition to having extensive knowledge about the peppers and other ingredients used in her dishes, she fervently supports any organic product, especially those that come from small family farms. Approximately 95 percent

Katharine Kagel is the chef and owner of Café Pasqual's in Santa Fe.

of the café's ingredients and the vast majority of the wines served are organic. "We believe in feeding our customers clean food," she says. "Not food that has been touched with anything that has *cide* in it, derived from Latin meaning 'killer.' Food shouldn't slowly kill people." She is also a strong supporter of buying as many items as she can from local farmers like Matt Romero when their produce is available in season. Everything at Café Pasqual's is made from scratch from the highest-quality ingredients and, in recognition, Café Pasqual's won the James Beard Foundation Award for America's Regional Classic in 1999.

In the late 1980s, Katharine saw a need in the community to feed those who were unable to find their next meals, especially children. Using all of the leftover food from the day at her restaurant and other local cafés and bakeries, she found agencies to which she could send their leftover food instead of throwing it out. In 1986, she helped found the Food Brigade and was later elected to the board of Foodchain. Today, the Santa Fe Depot, a local food bank (that evolved from the early days of the Food Brigade), delivers to over 135 agencies that support ten northern New Mexico counties by giving food to those in need.

Katharine, a proud supporter of local foods and artistry, opened a gallery around the corner from the café. Artists Felipe Ortega, Lorenzo Mendez, Marc Millovich and Yolanda Rawlings fill the gallery with their shimmery mica clay cookware. These clay cook pots are a traditional style of cookware that dates back to the 1500s and are made with volcanic clay that has naturally occurring mica. When the pots are fired, the mica melts, which makes it impervious to liquid. The cookware can be used on any stovetop, in any oven, placed over an open flame and even put in the microwave. When Katharine has guests in her home, she uses the shimmery clay pots to serve her salsa or chile sauces; they make perfect centerpieces that also have purpose. My favorite artwork in her gallery is by artist Rick Phelps, who makes a range of papier-mâché sculptures ranging from a life-size sculpture of a reclined woman to small sculptures of dinosaurs, piñatas, cigar boxes and many more. What is most interesting about his work is that all of his sculptures are up-cycled from various types of paper, which makes them enjoyable to look at for hours on end.

Katharine has a strong sense of the importance chile has had on what dishes she creates, on the role it plays in her life and, most importantly, on the culture as a whole. "Chile is life. It's good for you, it's packed with vitamins, it makes you feel good and there is a range of heat levels. Why wouldn't you want to eat chile?"

HARRY'S ROADHOUSE: A LOCAL HANGOUT HAVEN

Harry's Roadhouse is a local Santa Fe hangout. My family and I get together most weekends for breakfast at Harry's and have for many years now. As a family, we've rotated restaurants throughout the years for Sunday morning breakfast (usually frequenting the same place until we get completely burnt out...but that usually takes years). When I was a kid, it started with Tortilla Flats, followed by a succession of Santa Fe legends, including the Pantry, Tecolote, Tia Sophia's, Guadalupe Café, Bagelmania and Horseman's Haven. My parents liked the coffee at the Pantry and the quick service. Tecolote had an awesome "bakery basket" with mini cinnamon rolls that all of us would fight over. Tia's has some of the largest breakfast burritos in town for the best price. Guadalupe has homemade berry spread and cinnamon nut toast that pairs surprisingly well with the heat of its red chiles. Balgelmainia has hash browns smothered with red and green chiles and topped with cheddar cheese. Food in Santa Fe is easy because there are so many wonderful, world-class, delicious places to eat. In fact, sometimes the biggest battle is just figuring out where to dine. For now, our breakfast place is Harry's. One of the reasons we continue to go back after years of eating at the same place is the ever-changing (sometimes rotating) weekend specials. The

A classic breakfast burrito at Harry's Roadhouse in Santa Fe starts with a flour tortilla rolled around scrambled eggs, with apple wood–smoked bacon and potatoes topped with red and green chiles and melted cheese.

specials are a blend of New Mexican, Mexican and American styles of cuisine that are never boring. If we don't go for a dish on the specials menu, it's back to a classic breakfast burrito smothered in Christmas—and it hits the spot. Every time.

The great thing about living in a small town like Santa Fe is that when a restaurant becomes your go-to place, everyone starts to become more like family. Throughout the years of seeing the wait staff every weekend, you find out more about their lives beyond the food. What has become just as nourishing as eating is getting to know the people who have put love and care into the food they serve (or sharing the joke of the week). If we can, we always sit in Mary's section because she knows our drink order the second we walk through the door and our admiration for raspberry jam over any other flavor. Harry's, like a couple other restaurants in town, is about the crossroads and intersections of people of all varieties. The brightly colored walls reflect the bright, eclectic personalities walking through the door wearing sneakers, loafers, hiking boots, crocks—with requisite socks and shorts, of course—or fancy cowboy boots. Artwork varies month to month and showcases some of the best local work.

Harry's is about being able to eat a delicious meal and not have to break the bank. Harry's is about community and celebrating the "weird Santa Fe" in all of us. So what about Harry?

In 1971, Harry Shapiro left his native Philadelphia for a trip with a friend to Las Cruces, where he picked up a bag of dried red chiles as a souvenir. He was mesmerized by the earthy, sweet-spicy flavor and was instantly hooked. Over the years, he continued to experiment with chiles in a variety of dishes. Harry opened a Mexican restaurant called El Matate in Philadelphia, where he played with flavors and expanded his range of cuisine, but he eventually came to a point in his life when he wanted a change. He wanted to move someplace in the mountains because he loves to ski, but even more, he wanted to find a place that was a mix of diverse cultures. He left Philadelphia behind, made a leap of faith and moved out west to start a new restaurant. Harry and his wife, Peyton Young, opened Harry's Roadhouse in July 1992 in Santa Fe on a property that was once the location of an old gas station on Route 66.

"If we did twenty or thirty meals a day, we thought we had a good day," he says. Today, they do that much in half an hour. "You see a little bit of everyone here, and that's what makes it fun for us."

Harry Shapiro, owner of Harry's Roadhouse, on the patio of his restaurant in Santa Fe.

Since 1992, Peyton and Harry have stayed true to their mission of providing a quality, wholesome meal to whoever walks through the roadhouse doors. He finds chiles to be a source of inspiration in his work and still loves to taste the "different flavors more than anything, and that's one of the things chile does—it brings so many things to life."

Part V
THE INDUSTRIES

BOUNTY OF BUENO FOODS

For many fans of New Mexico chiles, few companies have saved us from having "chile withdrawals" more than Bueno Foods. I can remember the first time I was unable to get green chiles from my family's farm for an out-of-state Thanksgiving. I could feel my blood heating up at the thought of a turkey meal without chiles. A holiday—especially Thanksgiving—just doesn't feel right unless some form of red or green chile is on the table. On this particular day before Thanksgiving, I ran to the nearest grocery with a group of non–New Mexicans (all of whom thought my anxiety was unwarranted and that I was acting crazy for not settling for Tabasco hot sauce), and to my utter relief, I was able to find a frozen tub of Bueno Fire Roasted Green Chile that is certified New Mexican chile. I did a little happy dance in relief. The holiday was saved (for me, at least)! Up until that point, I had taken chiles for granted and had not realized the internal sadness I would feel at not having them. I realized that not having chiles meant I had no physical way to connect with my family and our heritage. Having chiles on the table wasn't so much about eating them as it was about feeling a connection to my family even though we weren't together.

I have certainly not been the first New Mexican to share these sentiments or to come to the realization that chiles should be shared year round and available outside New Mexico. In 1946, brothers Joe, Agustine and Raymond Baca, members of a longtime New Mexican family, had just returned home after World War II when they scraped together enough money to start a small grocery business in the South Valley of Albuquerque that they called the Ace Food Store. They quickly realized that the small business could not compete with larger chain groceries like Piggly Wiggly and Safeway, so they began to think of ways to make their business successful. In a burst of inspiration, they began to incorporate their mother Filomena Baca's New Mexican style of cooking into their business as a carryout component to the store. These homemade traditional dishes were a hit in the community, but the brothers realized that this business model couldn't sustain them forever, so they started to branch out, with new partnerships manufacturing tamales, posole and corn and flour tortillas.

It was the early 1950s when more and more people were starting to purchase freezers for their homes, and a light bulb went off in the Baca family heads. The brothers talked endlessly of how they could take their heritage and preserve it, so to speak. The idea started with the New Mexican tradition of fire roasting green chiles over an open flame and freezing them to last until the next year's harvest so that people could enjoy fire-roasted chile year round. There was no technology built or engineered that had ever processed mass quantities of chile in this way; thus, the Baca brothers had to invent the process themselves and find a way to build the equipment. In 1951, Bueno Foods was born, selling frozen chile products to the community year round. For over sixty-three years, the Baca family has continued to be a family-operated business and now employs over 215 full-time employees, with an additional 120 to 150 employees during peak seasons. Bueno Foods is one of the largest frozen green chile producers in the country, and you can find its products in many states in the United States. It was also the first company to become New Mexico Chile Certified (meaning that 100 percent of its chile and chile sauces are grown in New Mexico and independently audited and certified by the New Mexico Chile Association).

Ana Baca adds that her father always used to say he was "bred on red and weaned on green!" It's an understatement to say that chile is a core member of the Baca family and will continue to be for many generations. In Ana's words:

In our family, we grew up eating red chile from the time we were school age. Every Saturday, our mother made a double batch of her grandmother's red chile sauce. That evening, our father cooked up spare ribs braised in red chile. Wednesdays, we found comfort in our mother's beans and red chile sauce with tiny cubes of pork. Friday was enchilada night, and only the earliest risers got to indulge in the greatest of treats: cold enchiladas on Saturday

Packaged chiles from Bueno Foods. *Courtesy of Bueno Foods.*

morning! Our red chile suppers gave us many wonderful memories. Chile is our collective cultural heritage. We all have a chile memory. It unites us, it gives us joy, it gives us a unique identity that makes us proud of our culinary heritage. It's like sunshine. Can you imagine New Mexico without it?

GET LOST AT LOS POBLANOS

The warm May breeze blows through the lavender fields, delivering a sweet fragrance that delicately blends with the smells of flowers, cut grass and tilled earth under the awning of a John Gaw Meem–designed porch. Walking around the beautiful twenty-five-acre property at Los Poblanos Historic Inn and Organic Farm under the early summer sun will lead to another smell: your sweat. Sweat is an appropriate image to consider in the context of Los Poblanos, as generations of New Mexicans have transformed a rugged, high-desert environment into one of the state's lushest gems through a combination of vision, determination and commitment mixed with healthy doses of elbow grease. The story of Los Poblanos is the story of New Mexico—the story of America.

An organic field with bright wild flowers growing at Los Poblanos Historic Inn & Organic Farm in Albuquerque.

It is impossible to describe Los Poblanos without describing the people responsible for its success, and none stands out more than its original matriarch. There are women throughout history who have marched to the beat of their own drums, accomplished things that were unconventional (even deemed impossible) at the time and made lasting impacts on their communities that echo down through generations. One of these women is Ruth Hanna McCormick Simms. Simms was born in Cleveland, Ohio, in 1880, the daughter of a U.S. senator. In her early adult life, she owned and operated a dairy and breeding farm in Illinois, was the publisher and president of the Rockford Consolidated Newspapers and was a strong member of the women's suffrage movement, producing a highly acclaimed film about the cause. She also had three children with her first husband, who died in 1925. As a business owner and single mother inspired to make a more public difference, she became a U.S. congresswoman for Illinois from 1929 to 1931. In 1932, she married Albert Simms, a fellow U.S. congressman from New Mexico, and then moved with her family to an eight-hundred-acre ranch in northern Albuquerque that stretched from the crest of the Sandia Mountains to the muddy banks of the Rio Grande. This would become Los Poblanos.

In the 1930s, the Simmses commissioned John Gaw Meem (the region's foremost architect and "father of Santa Fe style") and numerous WPA artists and craftsmen to renovate the property's original ranch house and to create the Cultural Center, used for political and community events. Los Poblanos also boasted one of the finest purebred herds of Guernsey and Holstein cows in the Southwest and played a significant role in building up the dairy industry in New Mexico. This included helping to establish Creamland Dairies, an institution to anyone who has grown up in New Mexico. You would think Ruth might have been too busy for extra commitments, but in 1932, she founded Sandía School, a private day and boarding school for girls that would eventually become today's Sandia Preparatory School. Later, in 1938, she founded the Manzano Day School. Many years later, the Simms family donated a large quantity of land for Albuquerque Academy. Ruth also found the time to establish the Albuquerque Little Theatre. Education, agriculture, culture and art were undoubtedly very important to the Simms family, as Ruth and Albert endeavored to plant the roots of progress in the community as deep as those of the cottonwood trees on their property.

Los Poblanos may have shrunk in size over the years to make way for Albuquerque's northern expansion, but its impact on local farming practices remains apparent. The owners of Los Poblanos honor the history of the location with a commitment to traditional, organic farming that focuses on local land race varieties. These practices make the farm a USDA Certified Organic Farm and create biodiverse and sustainable alternatives to supermarket foods. Many of the crops cultivated at Los Poblanos are listed as endangered by the RAFT Alliance, including Chimayó chiles, Magdalena big cheese squash and casaba melons (from nearby San Felipe and Santo Domingo Pueblos). Growing these and other local crop varieties honors centuries of New Mexican agricultural history.

In recognition of its history, Los Poblanos is recognized on both the New Mexico and National Registers of Historic Places. Los Poblanos is perhaps best known by foodies for La Merienda, a restaurant where locally sourced meats and produce are expertly transformed via slow food movement methodologies into amazing gourmet masterpieces that "wander the line between rugged and refined." I'm not alone in boasting about their food, as the prestigious James Beard Foundation has given numerous recognitions to La Merienda and its current head chef, Jonathan Perno. Perno is a native

Traditional organic dried chile blends are sold at the farm shop at Los Poblanos Historic Inn & Organic Farm, in addition to an assortment of other local goodies.

New Mexican and an advocate of the farm-to-table philosophy. Dinner is selected from a rotating, seasonal menu and is served in a charming and intimate dining room by reservation only (it's a good idea to book well in advance). While the dishes are not generally chile focused, many different chile varietals (fresh and dried) make their way into the dishes to give a uniquely New Mexican spin on haute cuisine. Come hungry for dinner or with a sense of adventure to explore the grounds. Los Poblanos is a must for lovers of tradition, history and good eats!

New Mexico Chile Labeling

In France, certain types of foods are granted French Appellation d'Origine Contrôlée (AOC). This gives recognition to a strict group of foods that can be labeled a certain name only according to their terroirs. An example would be champagne or Muenster cheese; these products can be labeled as such only if they are a product of a certain region. Having this label gives the product a higher selling value and helps small regional farmers maintain their traditions. Several other countries have similar government-regulated certifications for foods. In the United States, we rely on labeling from the processor or the corporation to convey information about where foods are coming from. This doesn't necessarily mean our foods are "fact checked" by a separate organization. However, in the United States, there are solutions for how to regulate and properly label a specialty crop like Hatch or Chimayó chiles. Given the rising popularity and notoriety of chiles produced in New Mexico, labeling chiles as "New Mexico chiles" has become an important way for local businesses to differentiate their product and earn a premium over their non–New Mexican competitors. Chimayó Chile Farmers had a certification mark for heritage red chile grown in Chimayó, according to the U.S. Patent and Trademark Office. However, inscrutable companies that sell chiles not grown in New Mexico started labeling their product as New Mexico chiles as well.

According to Duncan Hilchey of New Leaf Publishing:

> *The United States has a variety of mechanisms to protect designations of origin for U.S. products. For example, at the federal level, "Vidalia" for onions, "Idaho" for potatoes and "Florida" for citrus are protected as U.S. certification marks. In fact, the owners of these marks are the state entities that control the production of the products and those who can use the certification mark via state regulations. However, the owner of a certification mark does not have to be a governmental body; it can be a private association or a cooperative.*

On June 17, 2011, the New Mexico Chile Advertising Act went into effect to combat this activity. The act states that it is unlawful for a person to knowingly advertise, describe, label or offer for sale a product as containing New Mexico chiles if the chile peppers in the product were not, in fact, grown in New Mexico. The regulatory program is enforceable only within state boundaries and works by prohibiting companies from identifying their chiles (or chile products) as being grown in New Mexico or one of its regions unless they have the proper paperwork for those claims on file with the New Mexico Department of Agriculture (NMDA). In 2012, the NMAC New Mexico Chile Labeling went into effect. This establishes the New Mexico chile advertising requirements for New Mexico chiles and products offered for sale containing New Mexico chiles. It also establishes a method of sale and record requirements.

The enforcement teeth for this program lie in the NMDA's ability to remove from store shelves products in violation. When the program was first introduced, that enforcement step was a last resort; instead, the NMDA has worked to inform companies about the new law and how they can comply with it. While these efforts have stemmed from wanting to preserve and promote New Mexico chiles, many chile processors have found the process difficult and have had to take New Mexico chile products off grocery shelves until they can go through the process of filing their paperwork. However, the program helped the NMDA discover how much money is spent on chiles in the state. In addition, this effort led to a newer program developed to create a trademark and logo that chile vendors can use to promote their products.

The New Mexico Certified Chile program (created and now funded by members of the state's chile sector) is a promotion program backed by a federal trademark. It works by identifying chiles (and chile products) as

The state chile sector–funded New Mexico Certified Chile identifies chiles (and chile products) as New Mexico grown so that consumers know the origin of the product. *Courtesy of the New Mexico Certified Chile Program.*

being grown in New Mexico. The program is informed by the same logic that informs Florida oranges and Vidalia onions—if a region has a great product, that region should trademark that product so it can ultimately fetch a higher price.

Beyond the administration and enforcement of the chile labeling law, the NMDA is now more than ten years into the "Get Your Fix" campaign. You can find New Mexico green chiles in more than two thousand locations of thirty to thirty-five retail chains across the country during August and September. NMDA's role is to educate store managers about New Mexico chiles; it teaches them how to roast it and sample it in various dishes to demonstrate its versatility. The store managers then share that information with their staff, who set out to incorporate the chiles into items across the different departments—adding it to pasta salads in the deli section and to breads in the bakery section, for instance. Public information officer for NMDA Katie Goetz shares, "I helped out with a few roasting events in Portland in 2011. I remember seeing salmon burger patties containing New Mexico green chiles at a Whole Foods store there." These types of events help introduce New Mexican chile into regional cuisines across the country.

Of course, there is a fee that comes with putting a New Mexico–certified chile logo on your product. Growers pay $500 a year to have their red and green chiles certified as New Mexico grown and to be able to use the label on their products. Many New Mexican chile processors struggle to see the benefits when they have already grown and processed chiles in New Mexico for the better half of a century, and their customers know that. Then there are the small, family-operated farms that struggle to make any type of profit as it is and are unable to spare the expense to pay for any kind of labeling. New labeling incentives bring up a broader question: does labeling New Mexican chile products as being from New Mexico have a positive correlation to the amount of chile acreage farmed? While these programs are still too young to tell if they will help increase the amount of chile acreage farmed or the amount of New Mexican chiles processed, they appear to be a step in the right direction. One thing is for certain: more Americans know of "Hatch chile" and "New Mexican chile" than ever before. As New Mexican chiles reach a larger demographic, my hope is that these new consumers will value their colorful cultural and historic heritage.

MEET THE SOUTHWEST AT THE SANTA FE SCHOOL OF COOKING

Have you ever had an idea that felt too right not to pursue? Have you ever thought, "What if I listen to that little voice in the back of my head and chase a dream?" Well, that's what happened in 1989 to Susan Curtis, who was going thorough a type of midlife crisis as she jotted down a list of ideas she thought would be fun to chase. She had retired from her day job but yearned for another project to work on, one that would make food a bigger part of her life. As she jotted down ideas of what she thought she could do, she decided that trying to open a cooking school or writing a cookbook would be the most fun. In her vision, the fun would not just be for herself but would extend to her customers (or "guests," as she refers to them), as well as to her daughter, Nicole Curtis Ammerman, who would become the director of operations of the business. Raised on a ranch in Idaho with a family that appreciated the importance of knowing how to plant, grow and craft dishes with various foods, Curtis had the tools to chase her foodie dream. She was well acquainted with working with farmers and bringing their foods directly to the table. From the start, her mission was to use as many local ingredients and New Mexican chefs as possible to teach and celebrate the joy of learning to cook with new and unique foods.

Southwest cuisine was beginning to boom around this time, and Susan's business took off. A couple years later, she achieved her dream of writing a cookbook and has now released four (working with her daughter on two of them). In 1993, her daughter joined her in the operations of the business, and the dynamic duo has forged ahead, making the Santa Fe School of Cooking a unique and celebratory experience. As a testament to the appeal of its classes, over 30 percent of its customers come back for multiple sessions, often planning long weekend getaways around the type of classes offered throughout the year. The mother-daughter team expresses that "we just have the best customers in the world, and that makes what we do easy. It's just a lot of fun cooking and eating with people."

The Santa Fe School of Cooking features walking food tours; a wide array of Southwest-centered cooking classes, like rellenos, tamales and burritos; a Southwest boot camp; and private events. The Santa Fe School of Cooking works with knowledgeable chefs who have specialized in Southwest cuisine, and classes begin with these chefs explaining the

Nicole and Susan Curtis are the mother-daughter dynamic duo that owns and operates the Santa Fe School of Cooking.

ingredients (their history and flavor profiles), then moving on to instruct the easiest and best way possible to make delicious meals at home. The environment is warm and inviting, as most people in the class are groups of families, clubs, friends, co-workers or just visitors (to ensure everyone is relaxed and festive, a glass of wine or two enhances the friendly atmosphere). After the chef has finished his demonstration/lesson, the guests are served the meal they watched made or helped prepare. The room always goes silent as everyone works through their first bites, then murmurs can be heard about how certain techniques really make a difference. Once everyone has finished satisfying their appetites, it's time to wander through the glorious gift shop, which offers all the artisanal local products any chef, home cook or foodie would be glad to receive.

During one of their boot camp classes, a group of visitors that consisted mainly of return students worked on mastering the difficult task of making homemade tamales, enchiladas and calabacitas. Even the most skilled *abuela* has a difficult time mastering the art of making hand-made tamales. The students are walked through the steps as the preparation and cooking begins. At the right time, the students are instructed on how

A completed entrée at the Santa Fe School of Cooking consisting of two tamales, calabacitas and a slice of red and green chile enchilada casserole.

to prepare the tamale, then fold, roll and tie it before cooking or steaming. At the end of the challenging class, students are reminded that although some dishes seem daunting, preparing your ingredients and organizing makes all the difference. I overheard a couple students note, "I could definitely make these enchiladas after work," and I thought, "That's what my mother and grandmother have been saying for decades."

Nicole and Susan invite their students to take a chance on chiles, promising that there is a pepper for everyone. "We encourage our students to try different chiles and to try different seasonings to make a different flavor." Nicole adds, "There is no wrong way to cook." I laugh and say, "But there are wrong flavors!" She continues, "Sure, there are certain flavors that don't blend well, but the fun of cooking is finding out what works for you and what doesn't. Hardly anyone get's it right the first time. Our classes get people more comfortable with Southwest ingredients, especially cooking with chiles." Chiles are one of the ingredients at the cooking school that they can never have a shortage of; sometimes, they bring in peppers grown at home or in the backyard of one of their guest chefs. Nicole shares that part of the chile's importance in the state is due to its survival in a high-altitude desert climate. "There aren't many things that grow well in New Mexico, and chile is one of those crops that grows really well here and, for the most part, thrives in this climate."

Noe Cano, the school's chef de cuisine, has learned a thing or two about chile over his seventeen-year span with the school. He shared with me that his car once broke down on a long stretch of desert highway, having overheated due to a hole in the radiator. Fortunately, he was on a road trip coming from New Mexico, and his car was filled with red chile powder. Luckily for him, he knew that the red chile, when heated to about two hundred degrees, would break down to a paste and then form a seal over the crack in the radiator. He ended up making it safely home—giving new meaning to the importance of chile.

Stories of food, especially chiles, having an impact on people's lives are what the Santa Fe School of Cooking is all about. Due to Susan's "midlife crisis," hundreds of people have discovered the joy of cooking with chiles. As a transplant New Mexican, she shares, "We certainly can have chile on every meal here. We like variety just like anywhere; we just prefer chile most of the time."

THE SANTA FE CHILE CHOCOLATE TRAIL

For years, consumers have seen an increase in the amount of snacks, candies, sweets and even beverages that celebrate chiles. In the United States, salsa products now rank as one of the top condiments. There's a host of items with chile as an ingredient beginning to command national attention. Some chile desserts and sweets sound strange to many—even to New Mexicans—but for thousands of years, Mesoamericans and their descendants have enjoyed the experience of chile and chocolate. For many, the combination is a match made in heaven and one that can easily be found throughout northern New Mexico on a trail some call the "Santa Fe Chile Chocolate Trail."

Kakawa

Kakawa, located off Paseo de Peralta in Santa Fe, is a chocolate store like few others in the world. Its specialty is serving a variety of historic pre-Colombian-style chocolate elixirs and a range of chocolate products.

Kakawa's cherry chile truffle, made with 80 percent dark chocolate, sweetened with agave and sprinkled with New Mexican red chile.

Originally from New York, owner Tony Bennett did extensive research on chocolate and combined this knowledge with local chiles, which he saw as important to New Mexican culture. He has recently added a green chile item to the chile-chocolate offerings. For locals and tourists, Kakawa is on the "must-do" list, presenting a range of spicy, traditional, floral and contemporary chocolates and sweets.

Founded in 2005, Kakawa gets its name from the same Mayan glyph from which the Spanish got the word *cacao*. The word the Spanish most likely heard was *cacahuatl*, meaning "sun beans," from the Aztec language Nahuatl. The Mesoamericans (including the Mayans and Aztecs) were consuming chocolate as a drink dating back at least 3,500 years. They considered chocolate—literally—to be the food of the gods. Spanish explorer Hernando Cortés is credited with bringing chocolate to the New World after he observed the preparation of a cacao drink in Montezuma's court. Like chile, chocolate was soon introduced to Europe, where its use and value as a commodity spread rapidly, becoming a core element in many European diets.

Kakawa's chile-chocolate offerings, excluding its chile elixirs, include:

- *Green chile caramel*: House-made agave caramel blended with dried New Mexican green chiles and then dipped in a house blend 80 percent dark chocolate; has a smoky-sweet flavor.
- *Red chile caramel*: A blend of six chiles from the Southwest and from Mexico stirred into house-made agave caramel, dipped into house blend 80 percent dark chocolate and then sprinkled with ancho chile powder.
- *Cherry chile truffle*: Made with Kakawa's house blend 80 percent dark chocolate; has a mild heat and tart aftertaste. This is one of the most popular items.
- *Chile dark chocolates molded in the shape of Mayan glyphs*: Made with Kakawa's house blend 80 percent dark chocolate.
- *Kakawa's chili blend*: Roasted organic chilies from New Mexico and Mexico and a rare chili from the northern Sonoran Desert.
- *Chile de Arbol*: Dipped in house-made agave caramel and then dipped in house blend 80 percent dark chocolate. This is the hottest item in the store; owner Tony Bennett says trying one is like "playing chile roulette. You never know what kind of heat you'll be biting into."

Whole-roasted Chile de Arbols dipped in Kakawa's house-made agave caramel and then finished with its house blend 80 percent dark chocolate.

Todos Santos

A beacon to passersby, there is a small storefront with a festive environment decked out with local artist Rick Phelps's papier-mâché artwork in Santa Fe. In every direction you look, there is something bright, possibly antique, folk-artsy and wild. The store is filled from top to bottom with color—a mannequin with Pez dispensers on every spare inch and, of course, chocolates that are some of the best in the country. In 1999, Hayward Simoneaux opened up Todos Santos, meaning "All Saints," in the Sena Plaza in Santa Fe.

Simmoneaux, originally from New Orleans, was a fashion student at Parsons School of Design when he took an opportunity to study in Paris. While abroad in Paris, he took an interest in old chocolate molds, which he thought were cool objects and often found at flea markets and antique stores. He started collecting them, not with the intention of ever using them, and then he happened to read an article about a guy who knew how to make them. "I called this guy and then studied how to make them," he says. Once he knew how to make his own chocolate molds, he thought, "Well, that would be cool. I could make anything and not be limited to bunny molds." He started working for a gold framer and learned how to apply gold and silver leaf to objects while at the same time becoming a self-taught chocolatier. "I could make molds of the *milagros* [traditional Mexican folk charms] that I had been collecting, and since I knew how to gold leaf and I knew twenty-three to twenty-four carat gold or silver leaf is edible, I just started making these chocolates that were gold leafed."

Simoneaux's gold- and silver-leafed chocolate products are one of a kind; they're made by hand and look like real metal and gold milagros rather than something made out of chocolate—a true art. He has been featured in several publications like *Vogue* and the *New York Times* and was recognized by *Chocolatier* magazine as one of the top ten artisan chocolatiers in the country. He has since expanded his chocolate repertoire and today makes a variety of chocolates, some of which consist of New Mexican chile because so many people were requesting chile chocolates. Most recently, he has teamed up with Katharine Kagel of Café Pasqual's and developed a goat's milk chocolate bar with pistachios, ancho chiles and salt flakes. Among his store's great selection, he offers a chocolate truffle with smoked pasilla chile and dusted with cocoa powder. One of his most popular chile chocolates is his dark chocolate, red chile and tangerine cream. Whatever your relationship with chocolate or sweets, you can be sure to find a match for your flavor profile at Todos Santos.

C.G. Higgins

Chuck Higgins has been making candy for over thirty-five years. It all started in 1982, when he participated in his first official event as a candy maker at the Minnesota Renaissance Festival in Shakopee. His peanut rolls were an instant success, and from there he traveled around the country participating in various state fairs. Chuck has been a participant at the New Mexico State Fair for over twenty years. He later opened "Chuck's Nuts," also known as the C.G. Higgins Candy Shop, and a café, both in Santa Fe. Chuck recounts his progress leading up to making chocolates, discussing the evolution of the craft:

Chuck Higgins greets customers with a bright smile at his sweet shop, C.G. Higgins, in Santa Fe.

Opposite: Hayward Simoneaux's chile-chocolate creations at Todos Santos in Santa Fe.

I kept avoiding chocolate for many years. I started with chocolate-dipped strawberries, then fudge and then the truffles, which aren't a traditional truffle because they're made with a fudge ganâche, which is infused with the various flavors. For example, the Fiesta Chocolate is ganâche infused with pecan flavor, cinnamon and then New Mexican red and green chile in the end. So when eating it, you get a wave of flavors starting with the chocolate, pecan, cinnamon and a little kick of chile in the end.

Chuck constantly rotates and introduces new flavors into the shop all the time. Listed below are some of his chile and chocolate creations:

* Raspberry chipotle truffle (my all-time favorite; I could eat one of these every day)

A hot mocha being poured, inspired by the Aztec tradition of mixing dried red chile powder with chocolate, at C.G. Higgins in Santa Fe.

- Santa Fe fiesta truffle
- Jalapeño lime truffle
- New Mexico chile truffle
- Chocolate chile fudge
- Red chile caramel corn
- Chile pistachio brittle
- Chile piñon brittle
- Chile pecan brittle
- Jalapeño chocolate fudge

Chuck's stores also offer a range of sipping chocolates. A flavorful New Mexican cocoa is made from an in-house chocolate blend, not cocoa powder. A single shot of espresso and red chile powder blended with ground-up roasted almonds and ground vanilla beans are steeped, strained and topped with whipping cream. I asked Chuck if getting used to New Mexican cuisine and eating chile had been an easy transition. He responded, "Before I moved here, not being a New Mexican, the closest thing we had to chile was cayenne pepper, so the joy of green chile has just been a revelation. Once you understand green chile—how to cook with it, enjoy it and eat it—you're never the same after that. I'm hooked!" And so are we on all of his sweet confections.

Señor Murphy's

Neil Murphy, a fourth-generation candy maker from Dublin, Ireland, came to New Mexico and opened a small artisanal candy shop in Santa Fe's Sena Plaza in 1971. Murphy was captivated by the local ingredients such as piñon nuts and chile and incorporated them into his signature products, which continue to be made by hand today. All of Señor Murphy's candies are made in small batches to ensure the freshest experience, and its toffees, brittles, caramels and fudges are made with as many local ingredients as possible, hand stirred in copper kettles, to provide the highest-quality taste and texture. Over the years, the staff's dedication to learning Murphy's techniques and recipes has helped the company grow and expand. It has moved to a larger location in Santa Fe and has six other retail stores in New Mexico. Some of its signature chile candies include:

- Dark chocolate raspberry creams with red chile
- Red and green chile jelly
- Roasted red chile piñon nuts
- Green and red chile pistachios

- Chocolate chile piñon brittle
- Chile pistachio bark
- Chile-seasoned pecans and peanuts (great for hikes and travel well)

Whether you enjoy trying a new kind of candy flavor or sticking with traditional types of sweets, Señor Murphy's has something for the kid in a candy shop in all of us.

ChocolateSmith

Chocolate pâté might not be a traditional type of chocolate bar, perhaps something to be found in a Belgian chocolatier, but in fact it started in Santa Fe. Kari Keenan had been working at ChocolateSmith when the owners offered her the opportunity to buy the business. She and her husband, Jeff, purchased it in the summer of 2005, bringing a unique twist to the Santa Fe chocolate scene. Many of their chocolates are hand dipped in Dutch cheese wax so that the chocolate pâté stays fresh and can be easily shipped around the United States. The chocolate pâté is different in that it's not made in the same way as a ganâche or a chocolate bark. Kari and Jeff offer a variety of shapes and sizes dipped in wax that can then be cut into just like a piece of cheese.

One of the chile chocolate pâtés that they dip in wax is the Sunset Orange. They start with 72 percent dark chocolate, adding New Mexican ancho and chipotle chile powder, along with orange oil and cinnamon. Other chile-chocolate options are:

- *Sierra Blanca*: white chocolate with lime blended with ancho chile ganâche and dipped in dark chocolate.
- *Mucho ancho chile pâté*: sold in chocolate squares or in a chile shape dipped in wax; it's a blend of 72 percent dark chocolate and ancho chile.
- *Pecos peanut butter*: organic peanut butter mixed with white chocolate and then blended with ancho and chipotle chile and dipped in dark chocolate; it tastes like a New Mexican spicy Reese's peanut butter cup.

ChocolateSmith also offers green and red chile pistachio bark, as well as red chile pecans and almonds. The couple is beginning to expand their business with a small location at the Santa Fe Farmers' Market Pavilion. Not content to rest solely on their chocolate laurels, Kari and Jeff also own Whoos Doughnut shop and will be opening a coffee cart near the Georgia O'Keefe Museum.

Part VI

THE PEOPLE

FABIAN GARCIA:
GRANDFATHER OF NEW MEXICAN CHILE

The "grandfather of New Mexican chile," Fabian Garcia developed the New Mexican pod type, sometimes mislabeled "Anaheim," in the late 1800s. Garcia was born in Chihuahua, Mexico, and became a naturalized citizen of the United States in 1889. He was a member of the first class (and was the first Hispanic) to graduate from New Mexico State University (NMSU) in 1894 (at the time called New Mexico College of Agricultural and Mechanic Arts). After graduating, he started his career at NMSU as an assistant in agriculture. Garcia went on to a year of special study at Cornell University in 1899–1900 and later graduated with his master's degree in 1906 from NMSU. Shortly after receiving his master's degree, he became a professor of horticulture at NMSU.

Garcia had the idea that if he could grow a chile that was a little milder, more uniform and better yielding, he could build it into a commercial crop. Before Garcia, chile plants had mainly been a backyard crop and were not grown on large acreage. He started to crossbreed three different varieties: chile pasilla (a longer, thin variety originating from Mexico), chile negro (a small, black chile found locally in New Mexico) and chile Colorado (another small, red local variety). He didn't actually begin crossbreeding until 1907. The official release year of New Mexico No. 9 wasn't until 1921. More than three hundred years had passed from the time the Spanish brought chile to

Left: Young Fabian Garcia. *New Mexico State University Library, Archives and Special Collections.*

Below: Mesilla Valley, circa 1940s. Workers pick chile in southern New Mexico. *New Mexico State University Library, Archives and Special Collections.*

New Mexico until Garcia developed the first New Mexican variety of chile. It took Garcia nine years to discover that No. 9 possessed the characteristics he desired for a commercial type of chile and was more resistant to chile wilt. The necessary documentation and hand drawings of the differences between the varieties throughout the season also contributed to the process taking longer than today's standard.

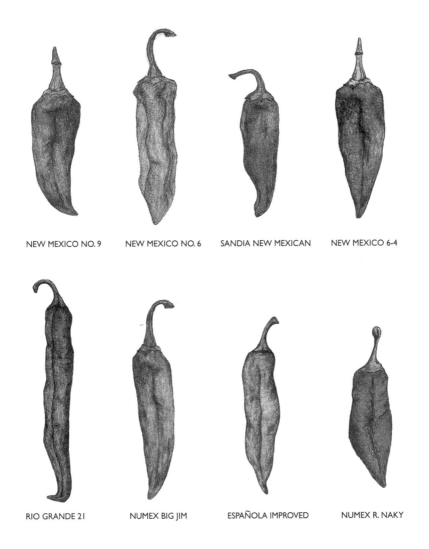

NEW MEXICO NO. 9   NEW MEXICO NO. 6   SANDIA NEW MEXICAN   NEW MEXICO 6-4

RIO GRANDE 21   NUMEX BIG JIM   ESPAÑOLA IMPROVED   NUMEX R. NAKY

Illustrations of NMSU chiles—some of the most common varieties grown in New Mexico from Fabian Garcia's No. 9 in 1921 to the present day (excluding holiday varieties).

New Mexico No. 9 was the very first chile pepper developed and released by NMSU. One of the reasons Garcia wanted to make a slightly milder variety was because he hoped non-Hispanics would start eating chiles. Garcia was able to create one pepper that was versatile and could be used for many different dishes. New Mexico No. 9 became the chile standard until the 1950s, serving as the base of many Mexican dishes consumed in the United States—like chile rellenos, salsa and enchiladas—instead of using many different varieties of peppers as would be done in Mexico. Dr. Garcia also experimented with and developed varieties of sweet onions, sugar beets and cotton and was part of a group that planted some of the very first pecan trees in the Mesilla Valley outside Las Cruces, New Mexico.

In the New Mexican chile pepper world, there is great reverence for the "grandfather of chile." Without Garcia's hard work and dedication to breeding, New Mexico might not have the commercial chile industry it does today. Dr. Garcia retired in 1945 after being diagnosed with Parkinson's disease. He passed away in 1948, leaving the entirety of his more than $85,000 estate to NMSU for "needy Hispanic youth." Garcia's New Mexico No. 9 was just the beginning of a very long and committed relationship NMSU would have with developing other varieties of chile peppers.

Between 1950 and 1967, Dr. Roy Harper released New Mexico No. 6 (later renamed New Mexico 6-4), Sandia and Rio Grande 21 (1956). New Mexico 6-4 is milder than No. 9 and is still a popular variety grown today. Likewise, Sandia is also a popular hot variety still grown today. Rio Grande 21 is hardly grown today, as the chile set poorly under hot temperatures.

DR. ROY NAKAYAMA AND THE FAMOUS BIG JIM

After Dr. Harper, some of the most renowned chiles to date were developed by Dr. Roy Nakayama. Nakayama grew up in a Japanese family that settled in the Mesilla Valley. He showed interest and enthusiasm in farming and raising livestock. Nakayama enlisted in the U.S. Army in 1942 and participated in the Battle of the Bulge. In December 1944, he was taken prisoner for seven months. Prejudice against Japanese people was common during this time throughout the country, and this prejudice was evident when he returned to New Mexico and was refused admittance to NMSU because of his race. Nakayama must have shown great promise because professors he'd had before the war demanded that he be accepted into the university. After graduating from NMSU, he went on to earn his master's degree from Iowa State College and his doctorate from Iowa State University. Nakayama, like Fabian Garcia, began to teach horticulture at NMSU in 1956.

It would be almost twenty years later, in 1975, when Nakayama released the NuMex Big Jim. The pepper was the result of blending a small Peruvian variety with Anaheim, native Chimayó and other New Mexican varieties. Jim Lytle, the pepper's namesake, gave much of his time and part of his land for Nakayama's chile breeding. Today, Lytle's son Jimmy Lytle and grandson Faron Lytle still farm the Big Jim variety of pepper on the same property. In fact, Jim Lytle holds the record for growing the world's largest chile pepper (a Big Jim), beating his mother's record at seventeen inches. The Big Jim variety has had unprecedented success since its release. The pepper has a medium to hot heat perfect for chile rellenos. It is milder than the Sandia but full of flavor. Big Jim chiles also have thicker meat, making them perfect for roasting. It's a variety that helped growers produce a higher yield per acre. The Big Jim also has a higher extractable red color than New Mexico 6-4, which makes it a perfect candidate for dried red exports in addition to green processing.

In 1984, Nakayama worked with Dr. Frank Matta and released Española Improved. This was a hybrid developed especially for the northern region of New Mexico and was created by crossing a northern New Mexican strain of chile and Sandia. Española Improved, like the northern land race chiles, was bred for an early and short growing season. In northern New Mexico, cooler nights start earlier than in the south, and the first frost will sometimes happen in September as a result. Española Improved is commonly found in northern farmers' markets as

Roy Nakayama stands in his fields with the chile peppers he has bred. *New Mexico State University Library, Archives and Special Collections.*

early as July and is grown in areas such as Española, Alcalde, Dixon and Chimayó. It has a higher heat than Big Jim but is comparable to the flavor of some northern land race varieties. It doesn't grow as long as Big Jim but roasts well and matures into excellent dried red pods perfect for ristras or chile powder.

In 1985, Nakayama and Matta worked together one last time to develop the NuMex R. Naky, named after Nakayama's wife, Rose. The pepper has a very mild flavor and bright red color, and because of its mildness, it is often used as a paprika cultivar to be turned into chile powder rather than as a commercial green chile product. In addition to his work with chiles, Nakayama also acted as one of the judges in the Annual International Chili Society Cooking Competition and developed two pecan types. He retired from NMSU in 1986 and passed away in 1988. In the year of his death, Dr. Mexal estimated that Nakayama's research was responsible for $10 million of New Mexico's annual GDP.

Dr. Paul Bosland:
The Reigning "Chileman" of New Mexico

If Dr. Fabian Garcia is considered the grandfather of the New Mexican chile industry, it is fair to say that Dr. Paul Bosland is the grandson and has done his predecessors proud. Bosland earned his bachelor's and master's from UC-Davis and went on to earn his PhD in plant breeding and plant genetics from the University of Wisconsin in 1986. That same year, he joined the faculty of NMSU in the Department of Horticulture. In 1988, Dr. Bosland, along with Drs. Jaime Iglesias and Steve Tanksley, released three new cultivars: NuMex Sunrise, NuMex Sunset and NuMex Eclipse. These three varieties are mainly used as ornamental chiles, making them ideal for ristras because they dehydrate sufficiently to eliminate rot. NuMex Centennial (in honor of NMSU's centennial) was another ornamental chile released in the same year and is intended to grow in small containers. The small pepper starts off purple and ripens to yellow, orange and, finally, red. It was the first cultivar released by NMSU that was a Piquin rather than a New Mexican pod type. Bosland then went on to co-found, in 1992, the Chile Pepper Institute, where he serves today as acting director. He became a full professor at NMSU in 1994, also leading the chile breeding and genetics research program.

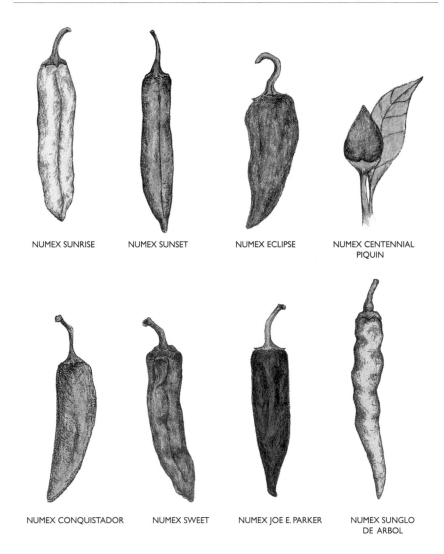

NUMEX SUNRISE   NUMEX SUNSET   NUMEX ECLIPSE   NUMEX CENTENNIAL PIQUIN

NUMEX CONQUISTADOR   NUMEX SWEET   NUMEX JOE E. PARKER   NUMEX SUNGLO DE ARBOL

Dr. Bosland's handiwork in the NMSU breeding program is evident as non–New Mexican pod types are introduced, starting with the first Piquin and de Arbol NMSU varieties.

To date, Dr. Bosland has released forty-two different chile varieties through NMSU, of which a dozen or so are holiday-named ornamental varieties. Dr. Bosland has been recognized for countless honors, awards and recognitions by universities, societies and councils. Thanks to Dr. Bosland and many hardworking researchers, the NMSU breeding program and the Chile Pepper

Chile Pepper Institute director Dr. Paul Bosland poses with one of the many chiles he has bred. *Courtesy of the Chile Pepper Institute.*

Institute are thriving. After having a long discussion with Dr. Bosland and several conversations with Danise Coon, a senior research specialist at the Chile Institute, I have never felt more in awe of scientists and agriculturalists. I was compelled to ask Dr. Bosland what he felt most proud of accomplishing. "I am most proud of the students I have touched," he said, "educating them about New Mexico's chile history and the importance of an education to their future." Dr. Bosland also spoke fondly of the NSF-funded ASSURED (Agricultural Science Summer and Research Education and Development) program, which graduated eighty students over the eight-year-long program: "The ASSURED program provided children of migrant farm workers the opportunity to experience agricultural research and learn the rewards and enjoyment that a career in agricultural research can provide."

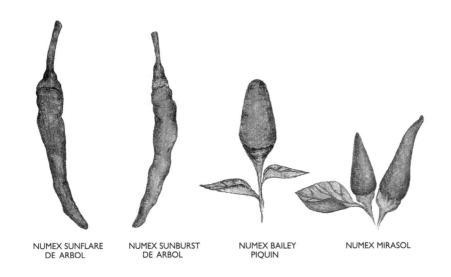

NUMEX SUNFLARE DE ARBOL

NUMEX SUNBURST DE ARBOL

NUMEX BAILEY PIQUIN

NUMEX MIRASOL

NUMEX TWILIGHT PIQUIN

NUMEX VAQUERO JALAPEÑO

NUMEX PIÑATA JALAPEÑO

NUMEX PRIMAVERA JALAPEÑO

Dr. Bosland releases the first NMSU jalapeño to help New Mexico compete with national and international canning and fresh distributors.

People from all over can come visit the Chile Pepper Institute Teaching Garden and view over 150 different varieties of chiles in the summer. By working hand in hand with **NMSU** and the community, the Chile Pepper Institute can help solve many chile-related problems. Dr. Bosland and his team realized several years ago that certain varieties were losing some of

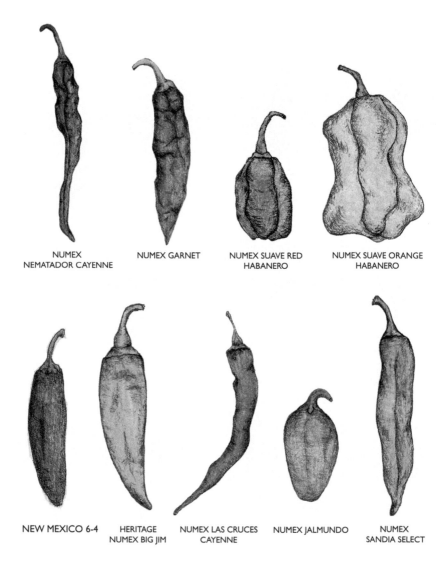

| NUMEX NEMATADOR CAYENNE | NUMEX GARNET | NUMEX SUAVE RED HABANERO | NUMEX SUAVE ORANGE HABANERO |

| NEW MEXICO 6-4 | HERITAGE NUMEX BIG JIM | NUMEX LAS CRUCES CAYENNE | NUMEX JALMUNDO | NUMEX SANDIA SELECT |

Dr. Bosland releases NMSU's first habañero and cayenne pepper varieties. Cayenne is excellent for dyes, and habaneros are perfect for hot sauces and salsas. The most recent variety of the Sandia Select gives New Mexicans a meaty green pepper with a consistent heat and excellent flavor when it matures.

their traditional flavor. They re-bred and developed the NMSU heritage varieties like Heritage NuMex Big Jim so that the flavor would remain consistent and the pods would be more uniform. What makes the Chile Pepper Institute and the NMSU breeding program so wonderful for the state of New Mexico is that they partner with local farmers, listening to their challenges and working with them to develop new varieties through natural selection to give famers a hardier cultivar that is naturally more resistant to diseases like chile wilt and chile rot. They do all of this with the hope that newer breeds will allow farmers to spray fewer chemicals and to use less fertilizer. It is a continuous cycle of getting feedback from the farmers, understanding climate changes and working on a cultivar that can thrive. A few years ago, they were able to sequence the genome of the chile pepper. This will help scientists study the genes of different varieties and observe characteristics that make certain strains naturally drought tolerant.

In more recent years, genetically modified organism (GMO) or genetically engineered (GE) produce has come under question, with many people concerned that there might be GE chile peppers being grown in New Mexico. Currently, there are no genetically engineered chile peppers in existence anywhere in the world, as researchers are unable to perfect the technique. This means that the peppers won't allow genetic transformation and are recalcitrant. NMSU is studying why chile is unable to go through genetic transformation, unlike its cousin the tomato. As previously stated, there are thousands of different varieties of chiles in existence, and all of this has been due to natural selection and hybridization, not genetic modification.

POPE OF PEPPERS

The rapidly expanding popularity of chile and spicy foods is due to many people; however, few have done more in New Mexico to promote a love of this humble plant than Dave DeWitt.

The first time I met Dave, he was wearing a bright, festive shirt adorned with hundreds of chile peppers and was casually observing the chile pepper plants around him at El Pinto Restaurant in Albuquerque. I didn't need someone to tell me who he was. He naturally projected the aura of "Pope of Peppers." I asked him if he could identify the peppers around him, and without hesitation, he started to list off their names, characteristics and how far along they were in maturity. You don't get the title "Pope of Peppers" without doing your homework.

When it comes to knowing anything capsicum related, Dave DeWitt reigns supreme on the subject matter (even on the rare occasions when his

Dave DeWitt, "Pope of Peppers," invites me into his library, where he often works on a variety of projects, many of which take the form of books on the subject of chile peppers.

encyclopedic knowledge has a gap, he can point you exactly in the direction you need to go to get the answer). He's devoted over forty years to writing about chiles and was *the* pioneer on the fiery food scene in New Mexico/the United States, founding *The Fiery Foods Show* and co-founding with Nancy Gerlach and Robert Spiegel *Chile Pepper* magazine in 1988.

Most would assume that he must have been born in New Mexico or the Southwest to have such a fascination with chile. However, Dave moved to New Mexico from Richmond, Virginia, in 1974, after having traveled to the state and trying his first spicy meal: a bowl of green chile stew. After sweating through the heat, he discovered how much he enjoyed the flavor and couldn't get enough of the whole New Mexican package (chile, culture and art.) He began his writing career penning articles and guidebooks about New Mexico, as he was fascinated with everything about the culture. Having owned audio and video production companies in Richmond, as well as in Albuquerque, he found an exciting, fun job writing, producing and hosting *Captain Space*, a Saturday-at-midnight show competing against *Star Trek* and *Saturday Night Live* and beating them both in ratings. While doing the show, chile became his niche topic of preference, and he ran with it, seeing very little work done by others in the field.

DeWitt relates his journey into the world of chile:

> *I realized early on that I had a chance to seize a niche—both intellectually and financially—that most people didn't even know existed thirty years ago: the chile pepper, fiery foods and barbecue industries. So I went multimedia with books, magazines, trade/consumer shows and the Internet…and it worked.*

DeWitt has written over fifty books; his first guidebook to New Mexico was just the beginning of a lengthy career as a food historian, chile expert and writer. But he didn't stop with writing about chile; after founding *The Fiery Foods Show*, he started the Scovie Awards, which now annually attracts over nine hundred entrants and more than eighty food professionals who judge the products and score them. He's also an associate professor at NMSU, has curated museum exhibits and has co-produced, written and hosted a video documentary. I had never met someone who was so completely immersed in everything chile. Dave takes being a chile head to a whole new level, but in a profoundly interesting way:

> *Capsaicin is only found in chile peppers and no other plant, animal or mineral substance in the world. All mammals, including human beings, have capsaicin receptors in their mouths and tongues, and what this means is that chile peppers and human beings co-evolved, and my theory is that they co-evolved to be domesticated so that mankind would plant them, ensuring that chile peppers have a wide, diverse group around the world, and since they couldn't reproduce themselves except for the small chiltepin types, it had to be mankind…twenty-five years ago most people thought there was only one type of heat for peppers and that was "kill ya," but today people know a lot more about the range of heats and the variety of flavors.*

DeWitt's successful books on peppers and fiery foods have educated the public to consider the pepper as a condiment or treat as opposed to something to be feared. Dave has been a huge contributor and advocate for chiles around the world, sharing his knowledge about them wherever possible—including chiles' elusive, perhaps addictive qualities. "While people aren't addicted to chile in a traditional sense," he says, "people don't go through physical withdrawals with chile, but they have a psychological addiction."

When asked about the cultural importance chile has on New Mexico, he points out that it's more than just cultural, historic and economic. "Chile peppers are almost a state of mind in New Mexico," he says.

It's a larger part of our culture; we grow more chile peppers than Texas and Arizona combined. In Texas, they have "Hatch Chile Festivals," and they worship it as much as we do now, especially the foodies. They even spell it correctly. Texans have a love affair with jalapeños going on. What makes our chile in New Mexico unique is that we don't add as many other additives like tomatoes or onions.

DeWitt sees the economic turmoil of the chile industry and an opportunity for change. He has plenty to say on the subject, as well as thoughts on what could help expand the declining chile acreage: "Chile season begins after the last frost and can start early to mid-April. The soil needs to be fifty-five to sixty degrees to start seeding. Farmers can transplant seedlings or directly seed in rows and furrows if they plan on using irrigation. It's more common now to be grown by drip." Drip systems are becoming more common considering New Mexico's drought situation, but they are vastly more expensive than using irrigation or well water. Drip can be problematic if you water the field the day before a large rainstorm; a storm could come though and drown the entire crop, killing it:

Farmers can use plastic instead of mulch with the drip underneath. The chiles are planted usually before May. They reach maturity in July and August. Fresh green chile season goes on for about two months. When the season begins to change, the chiles start to mature and turn red, and the plant beings to die. Chiles in the southern part of New Mexico can be harvested for red as late as December.

From beginning to end, it takes anywhere from eight to ten months to plant a crop of chile in New Mexico. This investment in time and resources comes at a cost. As I've mentioned before, there are several climate factors that play a role in the health of a chile crop throughout the season. Months of time and investment in chile can be wiped away in a matter of a couple hours if certain weather occurs. New developments and technologies are no match for Mother Nature. If climate factors don't affect the crop, then the farmer must take into account the competition from other countries that offer chile already processed at a much lower cost. DeWitt notes:

First, we have imports, many from Chihuahua. Chile is labor intensive; we always have a labor problem. Mexico doesn't have that problem.

We depend on migrant workers, and there are very stringent rules and regulations; there aren't those kinds of policies in Mexico, so they don't have to deal with all the same costs. Green chiles still all have to be picked by hand. You pick the chiles that are ripe, and the plant continues to grow more pods until the first freeze. Red chile is completely different; the plant is basically dead at that point, so you can use a mechanical picker that rips the entire plant out of the ground. While the chile pepper acreage has decreased, chile pepper production has increased. That means we've been doing more processing. Chiles from other states come in and get processed into dried, frozen or canned products.

If the New Mexican chile continues to decrease, the industry could become more dependent on processing chiles from out of the country and from other states. Every year, the chile pepper acreage decreases, but the need for chile throughout the Southwest hasn't decreased. More people are becoming fans of New Mexican chile; if only we could farm enough chiles to support their needs. I think there will always be a chile industry in New Mexico. We're still going to be making the foods that we have for four hundred years, but I think people are going to have to start looking at other

A small organic farm in the South Valley of Albuquerque that grows a variety of produce, as well as many of the popular "super hot" peppers, to sell locally and to interested distributors of the fiery peppers.

Bright, colorful peppers of all shades line the backyard at the home of Dave DeWitt, "Pope of Peppers," in Albuquerque.

varieties that are more valuable—like the super hots—and selling to private enterprises. I think diversification is the answer.

The most popular and valuable peppers on the market are Bhut Jolokia, Scorpion and Carolina Reaper. DeWitt is the first to admit that he is not a scientist and leaves the breeding to them; however, his thoughts and immense knowledge on chiles in the world are huge assets to our state and one of our most important economic crops. DeWitt is a busy man who always manages to make time for his wife, a beautiful pepper garden, two cats and his dog, Jagger. If peppers have taught him anything, it's to keep pursuing that next chapter in everything. There's always more to learn.

SALSA TWINS: JIM AND JOHN THOMAS

Dozens of old cottonwoods sway and swish in the warm New Mexican spring afternoon. An assortment of colorful flowers lines the walkway as vines dance along the adobe walls of the hacienda, where dozens of red chile ristras adorn the entrance to the El Pinto Restaurant (Spanish for "The Spot") in the North Valley of Albuquerque. As you walk in, the murmur of hundreds of guests fills the air, along with the sound of trickling water from the impressive indoor rock fountain and the outdoor Spanish fountains. The restaurant is filled with plants of all varieties, hanging and placed in every spare corner, and frames of famous politicians, musicians, actors and authors who have visited the New Mexican establishment adorn the walls. The patio of El Pinto channels the essence of being in a Spanish hacienda oasis, away from the desert life of New Mexico. Most days that are warm enough, the patio is chock-full of customers from all around the United States. On any given summer day, El Pinto serves anywhere from two to three thousand guests.

Jack Thomas, after returning home from World War II and taking time to recover from being held as a prisoner of war, decided to come to New Mexico using the GI Bill to enroll in engineering classes at New Mexico State University in Las Cruces. Jack met, fell in love with and married Connie Chavez-Griggs, a local from the nearby town of Mesilla, in 1948, after graduating with his engineering degree. They moved out east, where Jack found work for various prestigious engineering companies. Years went by, and they began to miss the food and sunny skies of New Mexico. Jack found an engineering job in Albuquerque, and with their six kids in tow, they moved to the North Valley, to a property close to the Rio Grande and out of the city.

The couple's desire to open a restaurant of their own came to fruition in June 1962, when they opened El Pinto. Connie Chavez-Griggs's parents had opened La Posta de Mesilla Restaurant in 1939 in Mesilla. La Posta was a quintessential New Mexican restaurant, and Connie learned famous New Mexican recipes there from her mother, Josephina, as well as becoming acquainted with cooking for large numbers of people. The restaurant was a family affair, with twin sons Jim and John washing dishes every Sunday. Unlike many children, something about the food and hospitality captivated the twins. When they were grown, Jim and John left home and worked in construction in Alaska for many years before they came to the realization that washing dishes at the restaurant wasn't all that bad; they missed the food, like their father had before them, and they missed the hospitality.

The twins came back in the early 1980s and began to learn from their parents, as well as improve on what they had created at the restaurant.

Over the next decade, Jack and Connie began to give full responsibility to the twins, who purchased the business in 1989. Today, the twins continue their family's tradition of serving New Mexican food at what has become the largest restaurant in New Mexico. Along the way, they began to see an unfilled need from their clientele, as several guests would ask if they could purchase a jar of their salsa. The twins saw this as a growing opportunity and worked to make their salsa available on grocery shelves. In 1999, the "Salsa Twins" released their first traditional-style canned salsa in a medium heat. Over the years, their salsa business has become enormously successful and won several Scovie Awards from the world's largest competition for fiery foods. Today, their products can be found in forty-eight states, and they jar as many as twenty-five thousand in one day. In recent years, the business has sold annually over two million jars of their salsa, enchilada sauces and red and green chile sauce. The twins were steadfast in their ideology of not incorporating preservatives into their salsa. They believe that in order to bring a quality product to the consumer, it needs to be fresh, and that means it isn't going to last for a year. As John says, "So many products say you can keep in a pantry, not even refrigerated, for one or two years. That doesn't sound right to me. Why would I want to eat something that is made to last that long?"

Jim and John enjoy what they do, learning from their parents that "quality food starts from the farm." Over the past several years, the twins have dedicated themselves to using the healthiest ingredients possible, as well as seeking to use as much local, organic produce as possible. They are committed to long-lasting partnerships with their farmers. For the past several years, Jim has researched and implemented methods that use scrap food waste from the restaurant for composting, relying on worms to produce leachate and beneficial microbes. This mixture, full of beneficial microbes, is sent to their partner's chile farm, where no herbicides, pesticides or fungicides are used on the plants.

The chile farm in southern New Mexico that they use is able to provide them with the quantity of chile needed to last the restaurant and salsa business an entire year. The hundreds of tons of chile are sent in refrigerated trucks to their warehouses, where their employees fire roast, peel and process the chile (either freezing or canning it). In one year, the restaurant purchases 1.5 million pounds of chile.

Beyond the daily bustle of the restaurant, the twins incorporate special traditions. Some of the traditions include Matanza, a traditional pig roast and summer music on the patio featuring local artists. These are widely

Marinated-to-perfection red chile ribs sit in front of a basket of hot sopaipillas and traditional El Pinto salsas.

Jim and John Thomas, nicknamed the "Salsa Twins," make three to four million jars of salsa a year and are the proud owners of El Pinto Restaurant & Cantina, located in the North Valley of Albuquerque.

popular in the community. Most recently, El Pinto has been featured on *Food Tech*, a show on the History Channel, and on *Ellen* for its "Yogarita" classes on Sundays. El Pinto is currently shopping around an idea for a reality show that would focus on daily activities of the large establishment. Whatever is next for the "Salsa Twins," you can bet it'll be spicy.

CHILE CHAMPION: LEONA MEDINA-TIEDE

Most people I know keep certain favorite food items on hand for emergency use. We stash away our favorite candy bars, savory treats or some other goodie for a special occasion or when things just don't work out the way they are supposed to. Everyone has his or her comfort food for these moments. As a kid, my special treat was one of Leona's flavored tortillas. I would beg my mother to go to a local Santa Fe grocery to buy a variety pack of these flavored tortillas as a reward for a good grade or some other achievement. I can still remember the excitement of opening a new bag and not knowing which one I would choose first. Would I choose the banana flavor and save the chocolate for last? The struggle was real, and oftentimes my indecision provoked my older brother to take a tortilla before me. Apple cinnamon (I almost always chose apple cinnamon first) was best when heated, providing deliciousness in every single gooey, sweet bite.

Most people think of flavored tortillas as a strange concept, assuming that all tortillas should taste of buttery wheat or corn. However, not all tortillas are created equal, and Leona was the reigning queen of all tortillas. Of course, I'm biased because of the wonderful memories associated with her tortillas. As a kid, I thought of Leona as a type of fairy godmother who made delicious treats for the children of New Mexico. It turns out that this was only half true. As a child, I didn't know whether Leona was a real person. In my mind, she was a myth of some sort, even though I knew she wasn't far away in Chimayó. A very unfortunate day came when I could no longer find these flavored tortillas anywhere in my hometown. I was told that part of the business had been sold, and it would be making only "regular" tortillas from then on. Leona's tortillas have become the taste of a beautiful childhood memory for me.

As an adult, I moved away from New Mexico for many years and was lucky if I could find any decent type of "regular" tortilla at the grocery store.

126

Leona Medina Tiede of Chimayó stands at the counter of Leona's Restaurante de Chimayó and Gift Shop, next door to El Santuario de Chimayó, where Leona once served delicious northern New Mexican cuisine that is famous throughout the state and country.

Then I moved back and remembered Leona. I needed to meet her. I needed to tell her what her tortillas meant to me as a child. Most of all, I wanted to taste her famous chile dishes at her restaurant in Chimayó right next to El Santuario. I remember jumping up with excitement when I talked to Leona on the phone five years ago to schedule a date for our interview. I was talking to the *real* Leona. It was as if Willy Wonka himself had answered my call and invited me to his chocolate factory. The day I met Leona was even more enchanting than the image I had concocted as a child of what she would be like. She was the real-life chile fairy godmother of Chimayó. She was around seventy years old when I met her, but she didn't look a day over fifty and had a wondrous twinkle in her eye. Little did I know that the day I met Leona would leave a lasting impression on my life.

Leona and her husband, Dennis, greeted me and were excited to show me around their restaurant and gift shop, even though it was jam-packed with tourists from Texas and the kitchen was in full use. Leona was born in Gerome, Arizona, the eldest of eleven children. After her father was done working in the mines when she was four years old, her parents moved back to Chimayó, to a piece of property next to El Santuario (a famous Catholic church and shrine). She grew up with her mother waking her and her siblings early in the mornings and teaching them how to hoe and till the garden. Her family depended on each member to get all the necessary work done. She learned from her mother that the best way to make any dish is to keep it simple. She would add only a little bit of garlic and salt to the rehydrated Chimayó chiles. This is how Leona would eventually make all of her dishes—the way she learned from her mother. "We were eating chile from the time we were six months old, so we never cared for the mild chile," she recalled. I asked her to tell me about her life before she opened up the restaurant, and she laughed. "Uh oh!" She paused. "[Before moving back,] it was one of the highlights of my life." Her husband Dennis gave her a look, and she added, "I said *one* of the highlights." They both laughed.

"The Santuario Church had always been a huge part of my life," Leona said, and she spent much of her free time as an adolescent working in the gift shop, playing the organ and volunteering however she could. "Since I was a little girl, I had wanted to be a nun." After completing high school, Leona joined the Carmelite nuns of San Diego. She was about to become a novice when she fell ill and decided to leave and return home. "I was called but not chosen," she said. After returning home, she took her mom to the doctor's office, where she was reading *Newsweek* magazine and saw a very small article about becoming a Pan American stewardess. She filled out the small questionnaire and sent it off "just for fun." Several weeks later, she received a thick yellow packet of forms from Pan Am. She completed them and mailed them back, and soon she was off to training in Florida for six weeks.

With Pan Am, Leona traveled to cities throughout South America, Central America, Europe and Southeast Asia. It was on one of her first flights to Cuba that they had to evacuate refugees. "We got as many as we could, twice a day," she recalled. She found out later that some of the refugees became Pan Am stewards and stewardess and would share their stories of leaving their families behind. This wasn't the only time she evacuated refugees. She transferred from Florida to San Francisco right before the Vietnam War. She was sent daily to evacuate refugees and return soldiers: "We would pick up soldiers for R&R and take them to Hawaii or Taiwan. We would feed them really well—large steaks, whatever we could. It was sad. A lot of them were the same age as me; they were very young."

On one of Leona's many trips to Honolulu, she met Dennis (who also worked for Pan Am at the time) outside a bus stop, and they were married in 1967. After the two lived and operated a restaurant in California for many years, they decided to move back to Chimayó with their three children. They first opened a roadside food stand in 1977 off Highway 76. Later, they moved to their final location (Leona's childhood home) next to El Santuario and converted the attached shed into a take-out restaurant. Leona and her husband expanded their business further by canning and selling her red chile sauce, as well as the same flour and flavored tortillas I knew and loved, delivering nearly twenty million a year in forty different varieties. If you visit Leona's Resteraunte de Chimayó today, you will find the walls filled with Leona's made-for-film life and the contributions and recognitions she and Dennis have made and received throughout the years. I asked Leona what her favorite item on her menu was, and she replied, "My tamale pie. We put a tamale in a bowl, open it up, smother it with pinto beans, chile, cheese, lettuce and tomato." Of course, her tamales are made fresh daily, offering vegetarian and chile-free options. "After traveling all over tasting foods from all over the world," she said, "I always preferred Chimayó chile and New Mexican food; of course, it was how I was raised."

After thirty-five years of cooking, in 2012 Leona closed the restaurant part of Resteraunte de Chimayó but kept the gift shop portion open, allowing her to get the rest her family wished for her. It was difficult for her to take a step back, as she fiercely enjoyed serving people, especially those who would make the pilgrimage to the historic Santuario shrine or come to taste her food (oftentimes, she would go the extra distance to provide an ingredient that wasn't on the menu). The long line out the door of her small restaurant was partly due to her inviting nature and long conversations to get to know the people who came to eat her food. Many times, she would serve the church in the mornings and return to the restaurant to work until close. It was easy to see that Leona's Resteraunte de Chimayó was an iconic spot for locals, travelers and the pilgrims of El Santuario.

When I think of New Mexico's unique chile culture, I always think of Leona—a woman who put spice into her community and every aspect of her life. Her patrons recognized that the excellence of her food was due to the love she put into it and the care she gave to strangers. Leona passed away in November 2014; however, Dennis and their grandchildren reopened and operate her restaurante, serving each meal in memory of Leona with the same love she put into every dish.

CHASING CHILE WITH CARMELLA PADILLA

Growing up in New Mexico, if you are sick, the first thing you do to soothe a cold is eat a bowl of chile. Carmella Padilla knows all too well about the physiological response to chile. She grew up in a family where her father was addicted to the hottest chile he could get his hands on; on the other hand, her mother preferred a milder chile. Carmella's upbringing—being a born and raised in Santa Fe—is what led her down the path of years of research. I met Carmella Padilla several years ago at her house in La Cienega, outside Santa Fe, near Rancho de Las Golondrinas. Her home is as artistic and diversely unique as the foods and flavors of New Mexico about which she has written. She is an accomplished, award-winning journalist and author. In 2009, she was a recipient of the New Mexico Governor's Award for Excellence in the Arts and the City of Santa Fe's 1996 Mayor's Award for Excellence in the Arts. From the first time I met Carmella, I knew we had a lot in common: a love of the arts, literature and New Mexican chile (of course). Her book *The Chile Chronicles: Tales of a New Mexico Harvest* helped guide me as I conducted some of the same research she had done and toured New Mexico close to twenty years after Carmella paved the way.

Author Carmella Padilla in her kitchen in La Cienega.

Carmella is an advocate for all things New Mexican and has worked hard to use her voice and journalistic abilities to promote and protect New Mexican farming, art, culture and traditions. She talked to me about her experience writing her chile book and how it gave her a deep appreciation for everything that went into a harvest of chile. She commented, "People sometimes complain about the cost of a sack of chile going up every year, sometimes twenty-five or thirty dollars for a sack instead of twenty, but they don't realize that is a bargain and oftentimes chile farmers are struggling to make a profit." Chile is planted in the spring (usually March or April) in southern New Mexico and late May in northern New Mexico. The first harvest in southern New Mexico isn't usually until July, as transplanted chile will start to ripen quicker. Therefore, farmers spend significant time and investment on a chile crop that won't usually see a return until mid-summer (and that's only if rain or hail hasn't come and wiped out the crop). Farming chile is a gamble, especially since chiles are a fragile crop to grow, made even more risky by today's ever-changing environment.

One example of the environmental changes in Hatch relates to water availability. Hatch was once a fertile valley with relatively abundant water resources; however, today many of the farmers have had to install expensive drip irrigation systems so they can ensure that their chiles get watered when they need to.

Carmella reiterates this point:

> *Farmers are staying true to a value that is lacking on the broader social level. Any type of farming has to do with an internal value system; being a farmer isn't considered sexy. People today want to get rich quick. That said, there are institutions and a mindset that has gained some steam that is about slow food, farm to table and overall supporting farmers.*

Chile through culture and through time has shown that its social and cultural value is more significant than its economic value. As Carmella told me, "Chile is always on the table year round no matter what the occasion." Choosing to farm chile, regardless of your family's farming history, is not an easy decision. Farming isn't as economically viable as it once was (and, as Carmella pointed out, it certainly isn't considered sexy). It's a career that most Americans take for granted, as foods have become easily accessible throughout the last fifty years and have separated the consumer from the farmer. The average person will never know who raised their cattle for the beef they eat or where any of their produce was grown. Modern Americans have largely forgotten the sacrifice and effort that go into the foods that give us sustenance. What Carmella and I have experienced by talking to farmers, processors and distributors of all different sizes is a profound gratitude for those who feed our country and give us our revered chile. Farmers, a lot like teachers, take on a career that nourishes the body, mind and soul of thousands yet go through life with little praise or thanks (more often hearing complaints about price), but they still feed us anyway. Talk about a labor of love.

When I asked Carmella about her thoughts on younger generations of farming families continuing the family business or looking elsewhere to make their livelihoods, she remembered her time working with the Lytle family in Hatch. Faron Lytle, the grandson of Big Jim Lytle, had to make a difficult decision: "He was in his late twenties, and he had an opportunity to be a pro-baseball pitcher and he consciously chose to stay and continue to farm. Today, it is a very successful farm, but not everyone would make the same decision."

It's farms like the Lytles' in Hatch that give New Mexico and Hatch a nationally and internationally acclaimed reputation for growing some of the best chile in the world. Chile, throughout New Mexico's history, has had this fascinating way of binding together local culture. I write this just as I've finished eating a red chile enchilada (the red chile coming from my family's Berridge farms in Hatch), and I wonder: when was the last time I thanked a farmer?

Part VII
FOOD AND DRINK

RECOMMENDED NEW MEXICAN CHILE PEPPERS

Extra Hot

For those who enjoy a lot of heat in a pepper—we're talking forehead-sweatin', mouth-burnin', eye-waterin' chile—I recommend trying or planting Barker's Hot or Lumbre chile. These are the hottest of the New Mexican Anaheim pod type. They can grow up to six to eight inches in length and have a medium-thick skin that works well with roasting.

Hot

These are some of my favorite peppers. They make for excellent hot chile for chile stews, as well as a chile rellenos where the heat can be balanced out with cheese and breading. Sandia, Sandia Select and Chimayó heirloom varieties provide a consistent hot heat when green and red and make for excellent dried red chile powder. NuMex Vaquero is a jalapeño providing a hot kick of heat in a smaller pepper, perfect for making salsas or as a taco topping.

A traditional chile relleno, like this one from Tune Up Café in Santa Fe, is topped with eggs over-easy, red chile, salsa and cheese, with beans on the side. This dish varies depending on the restaurant and its location in the state.

Medium to Medium Hot

Big Jim, Heritage Big Jim, Española Improved and Heritage 6-4—these peppers, specifically the Big Jims, can have a range of heat levels on one plant. When processed, it is best to blend with a milder variety if you don't want too much heat or to blend with a Sandia for a hotter heat. These peppers are designed for roasting, although the Espanola Improved typically grows the smallest and has the most heat out of the four varieties.

Mild

NuMex Conquistador and Joe E. Parker are two varieties that have a low-lying heat and are great for adding just a little bit of heat to any dish. I like to use Joe Parker when making Green Chile Cornbread or blended in with scalloped potatoes. These are the perfect peppers for those being introduced to New Mexican chile or for children who like spicy foods.

No Heat

There are a couple New Mexican chiles that truly have no heat. They're perfect for pan-frying with a little olive oil, spritzing with lime juice and sprinkling with salt or blending into salsas for their flavor and nutritional content. They are NuMex R. Naky and NuMex Sweet.

FROM SEED TO SAUCE: THE MANY WAYS CHILE IS PREPARED

When chiles mature, they change color. Most farmers and distributors will sell a sack of green chiles that might contain only a handful of red chiles or chiles that are a blend of red and green but not fully one color or the other. First green, the peppers change color and slowly turn red upon maturation,

Opposite: A handwritten sign from El Potrero Trading Post in Chimayó advertises traditionally hot chile.

sometimes while still on the plant. Starting in the fall with cooler night temperatures, the color and the chemical composition change. As the green fades, so, too, do its levels of vitamin C, replaced by increased levels of vitamin A; consequently, the flavor is different, too. As a chile pepper turns red, the "brix"—or the sugar content of the pepper—increases, giving more depth of flavor to a mature pepper. Once the color changes, the chile's shelf life decreases drastically. Think of the peppers like bananas. Some people prefer to eat bananas when there are no dark spots on the peel and the banana itself is not soft. Other people prefer bananas as they start to soften and the peel turns darker, but people who prefer bananas this way have less time to eat them before they go bad.

The most cost-effective way to enjoy the rich flavor of red chile is to dry it (on a ristra, which can last in a dry climate for years), grind the dried chiles into powder or turn the fresh pods into a sauce. For centuries, New Mexicans have set out their chiles to dry, the sun capturing—and to some, enhancing—their unique flavor for use in the year to come.

Roasted Chile

Roasting and "putting up chile," as most New Mexicans call it, is a daylong, labor-intensive ritual that is well worth the effort. Fire roasting chile spreads the heat of capsaicin located in the yellow vein, called the placental tissue, to the rest of the pepper. It is a common misconception that the seeds attached to the placental tissue also contain capsaicin. When a chile pod is roasted, the capsaicin oil coats the seeds as well as the rest of the pepper in a process called adsorption. Roasting chile also caramelizes the natural sugars for a more dynamic flavor in the finished product. Here in New Mexico, chile roasting typically begins in August (although it's becoming more common to see them earlier) and will continue through to October.

The most common method of chile roasting is to roast the chiles in a rotating, cylindrical metal cage above a fire. The cage roasters can roast around fifty-five pounds of chile (about a sack and a half). Fire roasting fresh green chile seals in the flavor and spreads the heat in a consistent way. Additionally, it makes peeling and storing chile for the winter a lot easier. It's important to freeze or refrigerate all roasted chile within two hours in freezer bags or containers and eliminate as much air as possible. Chile can stay frozen in airtight containers for up to a year.

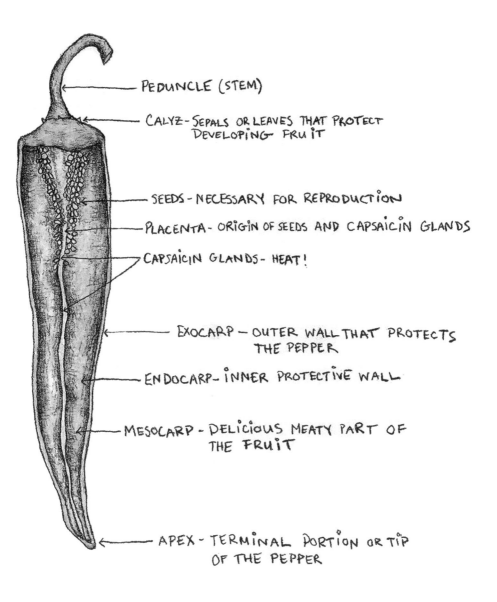

PEDUNCLE (STEM)

CALYZ - SEPALS OR LEAVES THAT PROTECT DEVELOPING FRUIT

SEEDS - NECESSARY FOR REPRODUCTION

PLACENTA - ORIGIN OF SEEDS AND CAPSAICIN GLANDS

CAPSAICIN GLANDS - HEAT!

EXOCARP - OUTER WALL THAT PROTECTS THE PEPPER

ENDOCARP - INNER PROTECTIVE WALL

MESOCARP - DELICIOUS MEATY PART OF THE FRUIT

APEX - TERMINAL PORTION OR TIP OF THE PEPPER

The anatomy of a chile pepper including the placental sack, where the capsaicin is located (note: capsaicin is not in the seeds).

What most non–New Mexicans don't know is that once chile is roasted, it needs to cool down before freezing. Putting the bag of roasted chile in a cooler filled with ice will help let the steam separate the skin from the meat of the

A chile roaster in action in Hatch, where every weekend—especially during the Hatch Chile Festival— storefronts on Franklin Street sell roasted chile to thousands of customers.

chiles, as well as eliminate bacteria before freezing. This cooling down process is really important because chile should not be put in the freezer if it is still hot from roasting; doing so can lead to sickness. If you are planning on peeling off the skin before putting the chiles in the freezer or refrigerator, the steaming process will make it easier. Many people who freeze their roasted chiles with the skin on find that it is just as easy to take off the skin after it is de-thawed.

The larger commercial distributors in New Mexico flash steam chiles, which is a much more convenient method for mass quantities. It allows the skin to be taken off mechanically rather than by hand. This is also a popular method for distributors who sell out of New Mexico. Some will argue that it changes the flavor to not fire roast and peel chiles, so many distributors also have fire-roasted versions for sale. There are certain distributors like Young Guns, a Hatch Valley company, that ship out their green chiles all over the United States and set up a chile roaster just like the ones from New Mexico, giving their customers the whole experience. By whole experience, I'm talking about the mouth-watering, mind-weakening smell of roasted chiles. I've been a New Mexican long enough to know that as a people, our two favorite smells are roasted chiles and rain. If our state's flag came scented, it would smell of roasted green chiles.

Green chiles are roasted at the Santa Fe School of Cooking so students can incorporate them into their calabacitas.

Fresh green chile can easily be roasted on an open grill or stovetop, although it is more difficult to equally roast the entire chile pod this way. Warning: the green chiles will pop, so I recommend making a small hole in each chile to avoid this. The Santa Fe School of Cooking sells stovetop-sized chile grills for dry roasting chiles and a variety of other vegetables. Another way of peeling the skin off chiles is to steam them in the microwave on high for about eight munities.

Green Chile Sauce

A green chile sauce typically starts with roasted and peeled chiles that have already been de-stemmed and the seeds removed. As I noted earlier, I like to make a couple quart-sized bags that have the already roasted, peeled and chopped chiles in them. I would take a bag of frozen chopped green chile and add diced onions and garlic. Some people like to make their green chile sauce similar to the way they make red chile sauce; that is to say, they start with a simple roux and then add the chopped green chile, then onions and garlic and whatever seasoning to taste. Some places will use flour, oil and a little seasoning as the base of the roux, and others will simply boil down the diced chile, adding a little oil. In some parts of the state, closer to the Colorado or Texas borders, it is more common to see pinto beans and even potatoes in the green chile sauce. To me, adding more things to a green chile sauce is halfway to a green chile stew, and I prefer to keep my two dishes separate.

The most common dishes to see green chile smothered over in New Mexico are any kind of burrito or enchilada. The green chile sauce is doused on top of the dish, covering it like gravy. Making a green chile sauce is an easy way to extend the life of frozen roasted chile, which most people buy to last them the entire year. Because fresh green chile is in season only in the later summer and fall months, it's nice to have frozen green chile sauce on stand-by during the winter.

It's worth mentioning that you can purchase dried green chile or dry green chile yourself at home. Drying green chile is a great way to make it last much longer, and it can be added to dishes throughout the year by rehydrating. Using dried green chile to make green chile sauce is easy. The first step is making a roux and then rehydrating the green chiles and adding them to the mixture. Dried green chiles tend to have more of a smoky flavor, which makes for a perfect addition to many soups and stews.

Red Chile

The "red chile" is similar to the green chile sauce found throughout the state, although typically more so in northern New Mexico. Red chile pods cooked in the chile Caribe style start with de-stemming and removing the seeds of dried red chile pods and then adding them to boiling water until the chiles are hydrated. Next, the chiles are put into some kind of blender until they reach the desired consistency; some people use a strainer to sift out the skin to avoid getting pulp caught in teeth. Once in a liquid state, some households or restaurant kitchens will choose to serve it without adding more ingredients. What is more common is to add the pure red chile to a roux of flour and oil, followed by garlic, garlic oil, salt, pepper and sometimes cumin and oregano to taste. I've found that red chile sauce in the northern regions of New Mexico has less added to it; many people prefer the earthy taste of red chile without added seasoning. In the southern region of the state (if red chile sauce is an option), it is more common to see cumin and oregano added. Making red chile sauce from dried chile powder (called "chile Colorado") is similar to chile Caribe but starts first with a roux; then

A traditional beef burrito smothered in red chile from Rancho de Chimayó in Chimayó.

Los Chileros distributes a variety of dried chile products, with every item well packaged and easy to find anywhere in New Mexico and at Whole Foods nationwide.

the chile powder and water are added slowly until the desired consistency is met. Red chile sauce made in this way has a tendency to taste more watered down and can be more difficult to bring to a gravy-type consistency.

Chopped or Whole

Asking for "chile" in New Mexico can also mean asking for diced green chiles that most people would hope have been roasted and peeled. Chopped chiles are added as a topping or integrated into every type of dish. Many restaurants throughout the state will also have the option to add whole green chile(s) to a dish. One popular example is ordering a "green chile cheeseburger"; you might ask for a whole chile on top of the burger instead of chopped chile. Ordering a burger or any dish with a whole chile will taste hotter for the simple reason that it still contains the vein.

Whole green chiles as a topping have become more popular in recent years. In fact, this past year at the Santa Fe Green Chile Cheeseburger Smackdown, the People's Choice Award went to the Mine Shaft Tavern burger with a half-pound black angus chuck, loaded with two whole chile

Above: Fresh green chile quiche from a small café called White Coyote in Truth or Consequences, a quiet town better known for its hot springs, artwork and being named after a game show.

Below: Jalapeño shooters, stuffed with three cheeses and apple wood smoked bacon, then coated in Japanese breadcrumbs and fried, sit on top of a cool cucumber dipping sauce at Coyote Café in Santa Fe.

rellenos, aged cheddar, chipotle dijonnaise and garnish, all on a brioche bun. This burger was one of two at the Smackdown that featured two whole rellenos as a topping on the burger.

Chili (aka Chile con Carne)

Well, let's start this off by saying that in New Mexico we eat chile, but if we feel like having chili, we make sure it's the best damn chili around. One of the main reasons New Mexicans spell chile the way we do is due to our Hispanic heritage, but it is also to differentiate chile from chili, or what most New Mexicans call *chile con carne*. One thing most New Mexicans are proud to declare is that in Texas, they eat chili, but here in New Mexico, we eat chile. Typically, chili contains some kind of ground meat, with beans (typically pinto), onions, sometimes potatoes and our New Mexican red chile sauce added to give the mixture some heat. Many places outside of New Mexico use a tomato sauce base that has dried chile powder in it to provide the heat. Chili recipes all over the country vary in many ways, as well as in heat levels. Here in New Mexico, we think of chile con carne as more of a mild, not-so-spicy side or the topping one would use to make a "Frito Pie" or smother onto a chili dog.

Frito Pie

The Frito Pie is a New Mexican specialty dish, and I'll admit it's more of a Tex Mex–style dish that is popular throughout the Southwest. The origins of the first Frito Pie are somewhat controversial, and there are two sides to the story. The first starts in 1932 with the founder of Fritos, Charles Elmer Doolin, in San Antonio, Texas. As the story goes, his mother, Daisy Doolin, made a type of casserole dish that consisted of Frito chips and a kind of Texas chili on top. The counter to that story starts with Teresa Hernández, who in the early 1960s worked the lunch counter at the Woolworth's (now Five and Dime) on the historic plaza in Santa Fe. She would get a bag of Fritos, cut the side open and add her recipe of chile con carne. Her recipe consisted of ground beef, New Mexican red chile, diced onions and cheese on top. Today, you can go to many restaurants and roadside stands and order a Frito Pie, the quintessential Southwestern comfort food.

A traditional Frito Pie sold at Five and Dime just off the historic plaza in Santa Fe.

CHILE DRINKS AND TREATS

Drinks

TEA CHIEÑO

William Zunkel, who has over forty years of experience living in South Africa, was well acquainted with rooibos tea and its health benefits. Years later, after moving to New Mexico and learning the health benefits of chile, an idea crept in. Zunkel kept seeing several flavored rooibos teas come on the market in the 1990s and thought why not experiment with combining the two. So he created Tea Chieño, which combines red chile powder with rooibos tea from South Africa. South African rooibos tea growers face many of the same challenges as New Mexican chile farmers, namely that their production is dwindling as they compete with other markets that can grow and process teas for a much lower cost. "The idea behind combining these two farming scenarios is to provide a 'value added' product that benefits both agricultural products," Zunkel says, "and Tea Chileño has secured sources of supply that fit those objectives nicely and in a healthy way." Tea Chileño can be found in select retail stores in Santa Fe or purchased online through the Chile Shop.

Tea Chileño is a blend of rooibos tea and New Mexican red chile created by Santa Fe local William Zunkel.

Chile can now be found in a wide range of adult beverages, including vodka, wine and beer.

ADULT BEVERAGES

Chile can now be found in a variety of adult beverages sold in any grocery or liquor store throughout the country. They range from St. Clair Winery Red & Green Chile Wine and Crater Lake Hatch Green Chile Vodka to Rio Grande Brewery Co. Chili Cerveza from Moriarty, New Mexico, and Crime a Lucky Bastard Ale put out by Stone Brewery from San Diego, California, which includes jalapeño, Black Naga, Trinidad Moruga Scorpion and Caribbean red hots aged in Kentucky bourbon barrels. It's also easy enough to infuse your favorite varieties of chile peppers into vodka and blend it with Taos-based Bloody Maria spicy bloody Mary mix. The chile craze, I would argue, has found its way into all aspects of the food and beverage industry.

Treats

One of the fun aspects of living in New Mexico is seeing how home cooks, bakers and chefs find new ways to use chile. One of my favorite local doughnut shops in Santa Fe, Whoos Doughnuts, owned by Kari and Jeff Keenan of ChocolateSmith, make a chocolate, red chile and maple bacon

A chocolate red chile bacon doughnut made by Santa Fe–based Whoos Doughnuts demonstrates the creative lengths New Mexicans will go to make chile a fusion food.

Decorative pieces made with dried red chile, corn and sage are common at farmers' markets throughout northern New Mexico and are sold to visitors and locals alike.

doughnut. Yes! Someone finally found a way to incorporate three of my favorite foods. While new ways of incorporating chile into foods are growing rapidly in New Mexico and around the country, I nevertheless enjoy the traditional style of chile cuisine. These "new" chile snacks are all about combining older traditions with new ideas—it's modern, fun and playful.

HEIDI'S ORGANIC RASPBERRY JAM

Have you ever gone raspberry picking and found that you didn't put any in the basket because you ate all the delicious berries right off the vine? Well, with Heidi's Raspberry Jams, you can enjoy that fresh raspberry flavor year round. Heidi Eleftheriou has a certified organic thirteen-acre farm in Corrales, five acres of which are devoted to growing her raspberries, along with some property in Los Lunas to keep up with the demand for her jams. Eleftheriou started first with a traditional raspberry jam and then branched out to Raspberry Ginger Jam, Raspberry Red Chile Jam, Raspberry Red Chile Ginger Jam and, most recently, Raspberry Lavender Jam. Each jam is made in a small batch, cooked slowly to maintain the natural color of the fruit, as well as its vitamin content. Heidi's jams can be found at most northern New Mexico farmers' markets or on her website at heidisraspberryjam.com.

Heidi's Organic Red Chile Raspberry Jam sells very well at the Santa Fe Farmers' Market.

I recommend a basic snack or appetizer where you spread goat's cheese or cream cheese on a tortilla, top it with Heidi's Raspberry Red Chile Jam, roll it up and then dice it into pinwheels. It's a perfect sunny afternoon snack.

OLD PECOS FOODS: DIANE AND MIKE JARAMILLO

Dianne Jaramillo was selling her Green Chile Mustard with her father, who sold chutney at local farmers' markets. Then she met Mike, who had been in the grocery business and knew how to get necessary barcodes and labels. In 1998, Mike began to work with his wife to help re-imagine her recipes and start to explore more gourmet flavors. Today, they boast Green Chile Mustard (top seller), Hickory Almond Mustard, Pecan Honey Mustard, Piñon Garlic Mustard, Red Chile Mustard and Spicy Garlic Mustard. "We like doing it because the locals love our products," Dianne says. "We get a lot of tourists that try it, then come back and vacation here and buy more every year." The couple makes the mustards by hand out of their kitchen in Glorieta on a weekly basis for the local farmers' markets and a couple stores that carry their products.

"I use the Green Chile Mustard to make salad dressings," Mike notes. "I love putting it on any sandwich and brats. It's good on almost anything. The Red Chile Mustard is particularly good on salmon, rubbing it on after it's been grilled with a little cracked pepper."

Assorted flavorful mustards from Old Pecos Foods are popular at New Mexican farmers' markets (especially the red and green chile mustards) and can be found at local specialty stores.

TALES FROM THE CHILE TRAIL

Traveling the "chile trail" has brought me great joy and a tremendous appreciation for the task of bringing food from farm to table. Of the countless pieces of advice I received from dozens of people involved in chile, the words of two people, a writer and a farmer, stick with me the most. The farmer asked me before I dove into a warm plate of red chile enchiladas to take a moment and think about all the things that had to come together for me to eat this meal. He told me to think about the red chiles and onions that have taken months to grow and then mature. Think about the people who took the time to harvest it and make it into a delicious sauce. Think about the cows from which you get your beef and cheese. Then take a moment to thank the animals, thank the earth and thank all the people who have come together for you.

This bit of advice has always stuck with me. Before every meal, no matter how rushed or excited I am to eat it, I take a moment to give a blessing of thanks. I feel nourished, mind, body and soul, by all the living beings that have sacrificed for me. Taking the time to appreciate food has taught me that working for the good of others is one of the best gifts you can give yourself.

The second piece of advice, this one from the writer, was that the greatest gift you can give another person is your time. It took many years for that one to really sink in, but I realized it was a driving force for my film and for writing this book. People gave me their time, and I took the time to listen. I listened to their passions, their hopes, their history and their fears. I found common ground with every person I interviewed, oftentimes over a

A chile-topped Volkswagen van demonstrates the variety of chile art, décor and style influence on the overall aesthetic of New Mexico and was a delight to find in Las Cruces.

meal we shared. The time I have spent learning their stories is priceless and something I would never trade.

The Zia symbol, a sign of unity with all things, is featured on our state flag. The center of the symbol is a circle that connects sixteen rays in four different directions, grouped in fours. Each line represents the four seasons of the year, the four directions, the four times of life and the four times in a day. All life is connected. Similarly, chile is one of the great unifiers of New Mexico. It unites us by a shared history, a shared enjoyment, giving us all a collective memory and a sense of pride. The greatest aspect of having this sense of pride in our chile is our willingness to share it and embrace those, regardless of background, into our New Mexican family.

This chile trail I have been on has given me the deepest sense of humility, respect and admiration for our beautiful state and our hospitable people. Chile is family, and I know that wherever the trails of life lead me, chile will always bring me back home.

Appendix B
RECIPES

Red Chile Beef Stew
Courtesy of Blanche Leone

Vegetable oil
1 pound beef stew meat
1 bunch cilantro
1 onion, diced
1–2 cups water
1 package dried red chile (seeds and stems removed)
Water, boiling
Garlic salt
Cornmeal (for a thicker stew)

Pour just enough oil to coat a heavy pot. Heat on medium. Add meat and brown all over. Add cilantro and onion, followed by one to two cups of water. Heat through until the broth of the mixture is a medium brown at the bottom of the pan.

While the meat cooks, prepare the sauce. In a blender, mix the chile, boiling water and garlic salt to taste. Add alternately more water or chiles until a smooth purée is formed. Add to pot and heat through for 20 minutes before serving. Add cornmeal for a thicker consistency.

Blanche Leone adds the red chile gravy she made from dried red chile pods to her beef stew for traditional New Mexican flavor.

Tomasita's Blue Corn Posole Stew

2 cups blue corn posole
1 cup pork, diced
1 tablespoon table salt
6 ounces onions, diced
1 tablespoon oregano
1 tablespoon granulated garlic

Cook posole, pork and salt. Sauté onions, oregano and garlic and combine with posole and pork. Adjust seasonings to taste.

• • • • • • • • • • • • • •

Harry's Breakfast Burrito (Serves 4)
Prep time: green chile, 30 minutes; red chile, 60 minutes
Turnout time: 5—10 minutes
Special equipment: blender and food mill for red chile

4 potatoes
Butter, enough to coat pan
8 slices bacon
8 eggs
4 8-inch flour tortillas
2—3 cups chile, red or green
2—3 cups cheese

Preheat oven to 350 degrees. Boil potatoes until soft. (We use Idaho russets, although some prefer red potatoes.) Let cool and dice into ¼- to ½-ich cubes.

Cook bacon. Scramble eggs, and when they start to set, fold in hot potatoes. Top with bacon and roll flour tortillas around the egg mix.

Top with chile and cheese and melt in the oven for about 2 to 3 minutes. Serve with a pickled jalapeño or your choice of garnishes. There are hundreds of variations on this dish.

Harry's Green Chile

1 onion, diced

1 clove garlic, diced

2 tablespoons vegetable oil

1 56-ounce package frozen mild green chiles, chopped (recommend Heritage NuMex 6-4, NuMex Joe E. Parker)

1 13-ounce package frozen hot green chiles, chopped (recommend Big Jim, Sandia or Alcalde Improved)

1 teaspoon Mexican oregano

6 cups water or stock, divided

1 to 1½ tablespoon(s) salt

¼ teaspoon pepper

3 tablespoons cornstarch

Sauté onion and garlic in oil in a large skillet until soft. Add green chiles, oregano, 5 cups of water or stock, salt and pepper and bring to a boil. Turn down heat and simmer for about 15 minutes.

Wisk together cornstarch and remaining 1 cup water or stock. Turn up the heat on the chile and whisk in the cornstarch mixture. Bring back to a boil and continue whisking for about 1 minute. Be sure there are no lumps. Simmer for about 5 more minutes. Add more salt and pepper to taste. The chile is ready to serve. It will store in the refrigerator for 1 week.

• • • • • • • • • • • • • •

John Sichler's Green Chile Sandwich

2 pieces multigrain bread

Mayonnaise

Roasted green chile, chopped

Tomatoes, peeled and diced

Onions, chopped

Slightly toast bread and spread on mayonnaise. Add chiles, tomatoes and onions. Assemble and enjoy!

Caldito de Calabacita Baca Family Recipe
Serves 8

The word caldito *is actually, in its literal New Mexican translation, a word for flattery. Yet many New Mexicans often refer to caldito (the diminutive form of* caldo*) to mean broth. For our family, however, a caldo or caldito was much more than a broth. It was a comfort food. Time and again, after entering the house on a cold, blustery winter's day or when we weren't feeling all that well, our mother would prepare a simple soup of vegetables, a little meat, green chile and spices, which melded together to create a savory broth that warmed us from the inside out. It also had the power to comfort us and to make us feel safe. Even now, this "little broth" can take us back to those times.*

> 1 tablespoon olive or canola oil
> 1 pound top sirloin or round steak, cubed (¼ to ½ inches)
> 1 large potato, peeled or unpeeled, cubed (½ inches)
> 2 small zucchini squashes, cubed (½ inches)
> ¼ cup unbleached flour
> ½ teaspoon ground cumin
> 1 teaspoon granulated garlic
> 3 cups water
> 6.5 ounces BUENO® Chopped Green Chile
> 1 teaspoon browning sauce (we used Kitchen Boquet® Browning & Seasoning Sauce)

Heat oil over medium high in a 2- to 3-quart saucepan or large skillet. Add meat, potato and zucchini and cook until browned, approximately 10 minutes. Stir periodically.

Stir in flour, cumin and garlic. Cook to brown flour, approximately 3 to 5 minutes. Add water.

Stir in green chile and browning sauce.

Simmer for 30 minutes or until cooked or desired consistency is achieved. If a thinner consistency is desired, stir in more water.

• • • • • • • • • • • • • •

Pope of Peppers "Icy-Hot Ice Cream"

2 tablespoon green chiltepins
1 quart vanilla ice cream

The thickness of protein casein in ice cream strips the capsaicin molecules off the mouth and tongue. Heat starts and then quickly dissipates as the ice cream and coldness come on.

· · · · · · · · · · · · · · · ·

El Pinto Red Chile Enchiladas

1 dozen 6-inch corn tortillas
1 16-ounce jar El Pinto red chile sauce
½ pound cooked meat (chicken, pork or beef), chopped, shredded or ground
2 cups cheddar cheese, shredded
½ cup sour cream (optional)

Preheat oven to 350 degrees Fahrenheit. Lightly fry corn tortillas in hot oil (steam for low-fat option). Put tortillas on a paper towel to drain excess oil.

Place a tortilla on a dinner plate, add preheated red chile, cooked meat and cheddar cheese (lightly sprinkled). Add another tortilla and build two more layers. Top with red chile and sprinkle more cheese on top.

Place in a preheated oven broiler until cheese is melted (approximately 5 minutes). Garnish with sour cream and serve.

For a traditional New Mexican favorite, cook an egg any style and place it on top of the enchilada. Serve with Spanish rice and pinto beans.

· · · · · · · · · · · · · · · ·

Green Chile Stew
Serves 12

A popular winter stew is the Green Chile Stew. Almost all New Mexican restaurants will serve a version of this dish. Katharine Kagel got this recipe from a close friend of hers, Greg Powell, a native of Santa Fe. Any variety of meat is fine to use: beef, pork, lamb, chicken or game. The recipe can easily be modified for vegetarian or vegan diets and is just as filling. It is a long cooking process with a lot of chopping and dicing, so be prepared for a 4-plus-hour commitment that is well worth the time investment, not to mention the lip-licking aromas emanating from the kitchen. The stew freezes well and can be kept frozen for up to two months.

¼ cup olive oil

2 yellow onions, diced

4 stalks celery, diced

4 cloves garlic, pressed

1 teaspoon dried oregano

1 tablespoon ground cumin

5 quarts chicken stock (you can get low-sodium organic stock from most groceries), divided

2 pounds pork butt

1 cup fresh corn kernels, cut from 1 to 2 ears of corn

2 pounds russet potatoes, cut into 1-inch chunks (no need to peel)

16 fresh New Mexican or Anaheim chiles, fire roasted, stemmed, peeled, seeded and cut into ½-inch squares (2 cups) or 1 ounce dried green chiles, rehydrated and chopped

¾ teaspoon sea salt

1 teaspoon freshly ground black pepper

12 corn or whole-wheat tortillas, warmed

In a lidded, 8-quart, heavy pot over medium heat, add the olive oil and let it heat up for a moment. To the pot, add the onion, celery, garlic and oregano. Sauté the vegetables, uncovered, until the onions are translucent. Put the cumin into a dry pan over low heat and toast it for 1 minute, stirring frequently until it is fragrant, and then add it to the stew pot, followed by 3 quarts of the stock. Cover the pot, bring to a boil, uncover, skim off any foam and then turn down the heat to medium-low. Add the pork and simmer gently,

Traditional green chile and pork stew from Café Pasqual's in Santa Fe is one of many traditional New Mexican comfort foods.

uncovered, over medium-low heat until the meat is tender, about 2½ to 3 hours. (You may need to add 1 quart of the remaining stock at this point if too much has evaporated.)

Transfer the pork to a bowl, leaving the stock in the pot. Skim any oil from the top and discard. When the meat is cool enough to handle, shred the meat and then coarsely chop it with a cleaver so the shreds are no more than 2 inches long. Return the meat to the stockpot and add the corn, potatoes, chiles and the remaining 1 quart of stock. Cook until the potatoes are fork-tender, about 30 minutes. Add the salt and pepper. Always serve this stew with warmed tortillas.

Appendix C

NEW MEXICO CHILE FESTIVALS AND EVENTS

NATIONAL FIERY FOODS AND BARBECUE SHOW

Where: Albuquerque (Sandia Resort and Casino)
When: March
Price: adults, $15; children ages 6 to 18, $5; children under 6 years, free
http://www.fieryfoodsshow.com

What to Expect

You will see thousands of the most devoted and crazed chile heads in the world at the Fiery Foods show. The show is now the largest and most visited spicy foods and barbecue show in the world. Founded by the "Pope of Peppers" Dave DeWitt, it has been around for nearly thirty years, with thousands of spicy products and foods to sample and learn about as the name would suggest. Each year there are approximately two hundred vendors selling chile, spices, barbecue and everything in between. Prepare yourself to taste the spiciest hot sauces in the world (followed by soothing ice cream) and attend fun cooking demonstrations from well-known local and international chefs.

Participants at the Fiery Foods Show in Albuquerque can get a little rowdy as people get their chile buzz on. *Wes Namen, courtesy of Sunbelt Archives.*

What Not to Miss

Every year, there are different cooking demonstrations that pair well with the selected year's theme and are always fun to watch. Arrive early when doors open to the general public, as people will be making a mad dash to taste their favorite products and make purchases. If you find a product that you like, it's best to get it right away before it sells out.

HATCH CHILE FESTIVAL

Where: Hatch (Municipal Airport, one mile west of town on Highway 26)
When: August (Labor Day weekend)
Price: $10 per car (this covers both days of the festival, so pack your car with
  friends and bring a large cooler and ice for fresh Hatch roasted chile)
http://www.hatchchilefest.com

The sign as you enter the town of Hatch announces Hatch as the "Chile Capital of the World" and that it's proud to sell you its chile.

Women ride on horseback and wear traditional Mexican fiesta dresses for the Hatch Chile Festival Parade.

What to Expect

Because Hatch is the "Chile Capital of the World," you can expect crowds. The current population of Hatch is around 1,600, but this tiny city packs in up to 30,000 during the chile festival. People from all over the United States make the trek to the Hatch Chile Festival every year to eat some of the best chile in the world. The festival starts off with the Hatch chile parade down Main Street. At the festival grounds, one can enjoy the chile cook-off, chile-eating contests, live music, a mechanical bull, a small waterpark and a carnival for children, as well as local artestry of all types. Did I mention the chile roasting? Several farmers from the Hatch Valley and the Mesilla Valley set up booths where you can buy sweet onions, ristras, salsas and the freshest green chile around (and have it roasted on the spot). No one year is ever the same as the last, but you can always count on a plethora of chile.

What Not to Miss

Rocio Bañuelos gives chile ristra–making demonstrations at the annual Hatch Chile Festival.

Ristra making: Every year, Rosio Bañuelos offers step-by-step instruction on how to make chile ristras. For me, this ristra tutorial is worth double the price of the entrance fee. Most vendors sell a single large ristra in Hatch for ten dollars. So if you can learn how to make your own and you buy fresh chile at the festival, you'll have a very useful skill that results in an afforable way to decorate your home or have "back up" chile to cook with in the winter. (*Note*: If you intend on eating the chile in your ristra and you use fresh green chile, make sure you put your ristra outside in the sun so it will dry properly and eliminate any mold. If you leave your chile ristra indoors, it will wilt and possibly mold as well.)

Former chile queens Lisa Terrazas and Selinda Alvarez-Garay stand with Jim Lytle and his mother, June Rutherford, as Jim wins the *Guinness Book of World Records*' award for the longest chile pepper, measuring seventeen inches long.

The Chile Queen and the Red and Green Chile Princess

Every year, the festival incorporates a Hatch Chile Queen and a Red and Green Chile Princess. These young ladies from the Hatch Valley are selected after giving public presentations on the selected topic for that year. Judges then score each girl on her presentation and select the queen and princesses. Each girl must be in high school and have good standing in the community. Throughout the season, the queen and princesses will be present in local parades to help promote the Hatch Chile Festival and the chile industry. At the Hatch Chile Festival, the queen and princesses collect a variety of goods (either homemade or donations from local businesses) and sell them to raise money to fund their educations. (However, these young ladies sometimes decide to donate these funds for local flood relief or other causes that provide financial aid to the Town of Hatch).

RED RIVER HOT CHILI DAYS AND COOL MOUNTAIN NIGHTS

Bluegrass and country music at the Red River Hot Chili Days, Cool Mountain Nights Music Festival and Chili Cook-off. *Courtesy of the Town of Red River.*

Where: Red River
(Brandenburg Park)
When: August
Price: varies (visit website)
http://www.redriver.org/
hotchilidays

What to Expect

This is a festival for those who love country, blues and folk music. Live music plays throughout the days and into the nights all weekend long. The festival isn't heavily crowded, but many of the bands will sell out before the festival, so it's best to buy tickets in advance. Red River loves barbecue and chili, so if you like listening to live music with a beer in one hand and a bowl of chili in the other and being surrounded by mountains, then this festival is the hoedown you've been waiting for.

What Not to Miss

The chili, barbecue and green chile cook-offs are sometimes just as popular and well attended as the concerts. These cook-offs are a fun way to get a taste of the many variations of chili, green chile and barbecue throughout the Southwest.

VIVA NEW MEXICO CHILE FESTIVAL

Where: Wagner Farms (1420 Desert Willow Road, Los Lunas)
When: August
Price: adults, $10; children ages 5 to 18, $5; children under 5, free
http://www.vivachilefestival.com

What to Expect

The VIVA New Mexico Chile Festival is located on the beautiful Wagner Farms, which has been growing chile and other produce since 1910, so you can bet there will be a lot of fresh chile being roasted and sold. The festival shows off musicians from around the Southwest, as well as a wide range of vendors selling New Mexican products. The festival also boasts a beer garden, corn maze, wine tasting and an assortment of activities for children. Hay rides around the grounds to see the different types of crops grown on Wagner Farms are another great option.

Beautiful vistas stretching 360 degrees to the great Sandia Peaks from chile farms in Los Lunas.

What Not to Miss

Who doesn't like checking out a mini petting zoo? I'll admit it was the first (and maybe the last time) I have ever seen a water buffalo and ostrich in the same cornfield—not your typical occurrence. They also set up an easy-to-navigate corn maze that leads to a small deck overlooking the crops and gorgeous New Mexican landscape. If you are looking for a family-friendly weekend festival and a place to expose children to the joys of growing food, then look no further.

FUZE SOUTHWEST FOOD AND FOLKLORE FESTIVAL

Where: Santa Fe (Museum of International Folk Art)
When: September
Price: registration $250 (portion is tax deductible); Sunday, free
http://fuzesw.museumofnewmexico.org

What to Expect

The mission of the Fuze Southwest Food and Folklore Festival is to study, celebrate and appreciate New Mexico's diverse cultures as expressed

Betty Fussell lectures at the Fuze Southwest event in Santa Fe. *Photo by Seth Roffman.*

through its diverse food, art and history. This is a weekend event for the devout foodie that focuses on conferences led by local, national and internationally acclaimed authors, historians, chefs, archaeologists, artists and museum curators. Each year, the conference covers a new topic that allows food enthusiasts to engage on new topics. Art breaks occur between lectures, with meals and snacks provided by local restaurants.

What Not to Miss

Sunday is free for the general public and is filled with a bounty of options. This is a definite plus if you can't make it to the entire weekend because Fuze Southwest and Delicious New Mexico organizes a selection of local food vendors, cooking demonstrations, artwork, gallery tours, presentations, music and dance. This qualifies it as the day to bring out the whole family and catch the fun.

SANTA FE WINE AND CHILE FIESTA

Where: Santa Fe (Opera House)
When: September (five days of events during the last weekend)
Price: prices vary depending on event; Grand Tasting, $150
http://www.santafewineandchile.org

What to Expect

Events throughout the festival include wine dinners, wine seminars, cooking demonstrations, guest chef lunches and tours, a gran fondo bike ride, the Gruet Golf Classic and the Grand Tasting. These events host locally and internationally acclaimed chefs paired with some of the best wines from around the world. No matter which event you choose, be prepared for some of the most delectable food and wines around.

Short rib marinated in Chimayó and Vietnamese Sambal red chile on top of cool coleslaw from chef Eric DiStefano of Geronimo's and Coyote Café at the Santa Fe Wine and Chile Fiesta.

What Not to Miss

Make sure to come hungry and thirsty for the Grand Tasting. It is the most popular event and sells out every year. It features over eighty local restaurants and around one hundred different wineries, all willing and eager to serve samples to the masses.

WHOLE ENCHILADA FIESTA

Where: Las Cruces (Meerscheidt Center Complex)
When: September (last weekend)
Price: adults, $10; children 12 and under, free
http://www.enchiladafiesta.com

What to Expect

This annual event is held at the Meerscheidt Center Complex in Las Cruces. Roberto Estrada is the event founder, and in 2000, he and his team won the *Guinness Book of World Records'* award for the largest three-layered enchilada. Roberto has been dishing up spicy New Mexican food since 1980. The event increases in size each year, as forty to sixty thousand people flock to see the making of the world's largest enchilada. The festival boasts the largest parade in New Mexico and incorporates local and national musicians, a 5K fun run, a plethora of food and vendor booths, activities and a carnival for children and an enchilada-eating contest. You can rest assured that there is something here for everyone.

What Not to Miss

The biggest reason to attend is to see the making of the world's largest enchilada. In case you were wondering, here are the ingredients:

Onions are sprinkled over the enchilada at the Whole Enchilada Fiesta in Las Cruces. *Photo by Sarah Traux.*

A small portion of the one-ton enchilada at the Whole Enchilada Fiesta showcases all the ingredients used in making the world's largest enchilada in Las Cruces. *Photo by Sarah Traux.*

750 pounds stone-ground corn (to make the Masa tortillas)
175 gallons vegetable oil, heated (to cook the tortillas)
75 gallons red chile sauce
175 pounds cheese, grated
50 pounds onions, chopped
48 heads lettuce, chopped
2 boxes tomatoes, sliced

The enchilada gets divvied out, and onlookers get to taste how the world's largest stacks up against their favorites.

GREEN CHILE CHEESEBURGER CHALLENGE

Where: Albuquerque (New Mexico State Fairgrounds)
When: September
Price: adults ages 12 to 64, $10; seniors ages 65 and up, $7; children ages 6 to 11, $7; little ones ages 0 to 5, free
http://exponm.com/things-to-do/green-chile-cheeseburger-challenge

Green chile cheeseburgers cooking before being served to the hungry crowd that has been anticipating this filling event.

What to Expect and What Not to Miss

This is an afternoon event at the New Mexico State Fair. Try samples from New Mexican vendors competing for the title of best green chile cheeseburger. Stick around to hear the judges and people's choice for the best green chile cheeseburger. The only rule is that New Mexican chile must be used.

GREEN CHILE CHEESEBURGER SMACKDOWN

Where: Santa Fe (Farmers' Market Pavilion)
When: September
Price: $20
http://santafe.org/Fun_Food_Event

What to Expect and What Not to Miss

Santa Fe is home to some of the most celebrated burgers in the entire country. Locals and visitors alike come to partake of the samplings offered by several local restaurants competing for the People's Choice Award and the Judges' Choice Award. Watch the chefs and staff of your favorite restaurant compete, and vote for your favorite green chile cheeseburger. You might want to come wearing stretchy pants because no one leaves hungry (#meatsweats).

Anasazi Restaurant sous-chef Julio Cabrera shows off a 100 percent Wagyu Burger topped with green chile chimichurri, provolone and avocado on a homemade pepper jack brioche bun.

Above: Some of the massive Mad Chile Burgers from Mine Shaft Tavern in Madrid being prepped for the Santa Fe Green Chile Cheeseburger Smackdown, where they won the People's Choice Award in 2014.

Right: Beatrice Archuleta strings up her beautiful red chiles from her family's farm in Dixon, New Mexico, at the Harvest Festival at Rancho de Las Golondrinas in La Cienega, New Mexico.

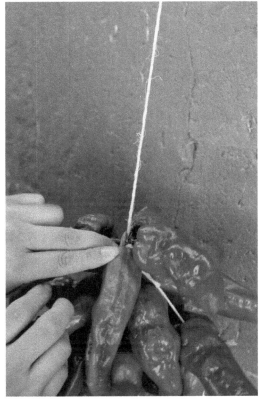

El Rancho de Las Golondrinas
Harvest Festival

Where: Santa Fe (El Rancho de Las Golondrinas, 334 Los Pinos Road)
When: October
Price: adults, $8; seniors ages 62 and older, $6; teens ages 13 to 18, $6;
   children ages 12 and under, free
http://golondrinas.org/

What to Expect

For those who like living history museums, this event is a must. Take a trip back in time and learn about what life was like for early New Mexican settlers during the eighteenth and nineteenth centuries. At the Harvest Festival, take part in stomping on grapes, learning how to string up a ristra, tortilla making and baking bread from a traditional *horno*.

The Archuleta women dress in traditional garb for the Harvest Festival at Rancho de Las Golondrinas and demonstrate to festival-goers how harvesting chile and making ristras hasn't changed all that much over the past couple centuries.

What Not to Miss

The Archuleta women from Dixon bring up red chile from their farm and demonstrate how to make ristras using their land race chile. Like many chile celebrations in New Mexico, it's a family affair, sometimes spanning three, four or five generations, where younger generations learn about traditions like how to make ristras for their own families.

ALBUQUERQUE INTERNATIONAL BALLOON FIESTA

Where: Albuquerque (Balloon Fiesta Park)
When: October (over ten days, including two weekends early in the month)
Price: adults, $8 per session; children ages 12 and under, free
http://www.balloonfiesta.com

What to Expect

Come witness more than five hundred hot-air balloons of all different shapes, sizes and colors take flight at the world's largest international balloon festival. Getting to and from Balloon Fiesta Park can be a challenge (leaving will take time because of every year's record attendance). The best advice for someone who has never attended the Balloon Fiesta is to arrive at the park around 6:00 or 6:30 a.m. wearing warm clothes and jackets. Expect traffic and delays going to and from the fiesta, as on peak days more than 100,000 people are in attendance. The balloons start to enlarge to take flight in the early morning as the sun rises, depending on weather. October weather in New Mexico can be fickle, so it is common to see one or two morning or evening balloon launches cancelled as a result. The Rodeo Glow (or Special Shapes Glow) is a balloon glow that takes place at night, with all of the balloons in special shapes like bumblebees, Darth Vader, Yoda and Angry Birds. Each year, the Balloon Fiesta is such a unique festival that it is difficult to draw comparisons with any previous year.

Above: Fall evenings twinkle bright with hot-air balloons during the Balloon Fiesta in Albuquerque.

Left: A chile pepper ristra hot-air balloon at the Albuquerque International Balloon Fiesta in 1997. *Chel Beeson, courtesy of Sunbelt Archives.*

What Not to Miss

I like to pick a balloon that is laid out on the grass and stand by and watch as the balloon team starts to blow it up. Energy around the balloon starts to buzz as people begin to cheer on the ballooning team, and within moments the ropes are untied and the balloon is off into the bright blue New Mexican sky. The only thing that can make a morning filled with hot-air balloons even better is a hot breakfast burrito with red or green chile. Every year, the festival food vendors increase (or at least it seems this way). Even after attending the Balloon Fiesta for over twenty years, I can say with confidence that I haven't sampled every vendor's burritos. Bueno Foods always puts out a truck where it gives samples of New Mexican roasted green chile on a tortilla. Grab a delicious green or red chile burrito, park yourself by a balloon and witness the excitement yourself—and maybe even go up in one if you're feeling adventurous. I did mention before that chile eaters are more likely to be risk takers.

LAS CRUCES CHILE DROP

Where: Las Cruces (Main Street)
When: December (New Year's Eve)
Price: free
http://www.lascruceschiledrop.com

What to Expect

Southern New Mexican residents flock to the main street of Las Cruces for New Year's Eve celebrations. The street is filled with fun for all ages, ranging from live concerts and theater performances throughout the evening, food truck vendors, children's arts and crafts provided by the West End Art Depot (aka WE.ad), beer and wine gardens for adults and, of course, the fifteen-foot chile drop.

What Not to Miss

Come early or stay late, but don't miss the fifteen-foot chile drop that flashes lights of all different colors as it inches closer to midnight. Take a guess at what color the pepper will be as it drops to the New Year: red or green?

A poster for the first annual New Year's Eve Chile Drop in Las Cruces, New Mexico. *Russ Smith, courtesy of Project Mainstreet.*

OTHER NOTABLE CHILE FESTIVALS

Albuquerque Old Town Salsa Fiesta, September
Sutherland Farms Green Chile Festival in Farmington, September
Taos Chile Challenge, September
Madrid Chile Festival, October
Silver City Tamale Fiesta, December

BIBLIOGRAPHY

Abbasi, Jennifer. "Love of Spicy Food Is Built into Your Personality." *Popular Science*, December 6, 2012.

American Spice Trade Association. "Method 20.1. Official Analytical Method." *http://www.popsci.com/science/article/2012-12/love-spicy-food-built-your-personality* (accessed February 14, 2015).

Associated Press. "Planted Chile Acreage Dropped 10 Percent in New Mexico." March 4, 2015.

Award Winning Recipes: Hatch Chile Festival. Hatch Chapter of the Family, Career and Community Leaders of America, 1996.

Bannerman, Ty. "A Myth, Hatched." *Alibi*, November 8, 2012.

Bannister, Justin. "NMSU Produces Super-Flavored Chile." *NMSU Research and Resources Magazine* (Spring 2010).

———. "NMSU's Chile Pepper Institute Debuts Limited Edition NuMex Heritage 6-4 Red Chile Powder." NMSU News Center, January 12, 2015.

———. "NMSU's Chile Pepper Institute Goes from Red to Green with Latest Variety: NuMex Sandia Select." NMSU News Center, January 6, 2014.

———. "NMSU's Chile Pepper Institute Names the Trinidad Moruga Scorpion Hottest Pepper on Earth." NMSU News Center, February 13, 2012.

Bonné, Jon. "10 More Foods that Make America Great: Frito Pie." Msnbc.com, July 7, 2006.

Bosland, Paul. "Chiles: A Diverse Crop." *HortTechnology*, 1992.

———. "Fabián García—Pioneer Hispanic Horticulturist." Chile Pepper Institute, n.d.

———. "'NuMex Heritage 6-4' New Mexican Chile Pepper." *HortScience*, April 2, 2012.

———. "'NuMex Sunglo,' 'NuMex Sunflare,' 'NuMex Sunburst' Ornamental Chile Peppers." *HortScience*, 1992.

BIBLIOGRAPHY

Bosland, Paul, Alton Bailey and Jaime Iglesias. *Capsicum Pepper Varieties and Classification*. Las Cruces: New Mexico State University Cooperative Extension Service, 1988.

Bosland, Paul, and Eric Votava. *Notice of the Naming and Release of 'NuMex Vaquero,' a High-Yielding Jalapeño*. Las Cruces: New Mexico State University Agricultural Experiment Station, 1997.

———. "'NuMex Primavera' Jalapeño." *HortScience*, 1998.

———. "'NuMex Suave Red' and 'NuMex Suave Orange' Mild Capsicum Chinese Cultivars." *HortScience*, 2004.

Bosland, Paul, and Jaime Iglesias. "'NuMex Bailey Piquin' Chile pepper." *HortScience*, 1992.

Bosland, Paul, and Max Gonzalez. "'NuMex Mirasol' Chile." *HortScience*, 1994.

Bosland, Paul, Jaime Iglesias and Max Gonzalez. "'NuMex Centennial' and 'NuMex Twilight' Ornamental Chiles." *HortScience*, 1994.

———. "'NuMex Joe E. Parker' Chile." *HortScience*, 1993.

———. "'NuMex Sweet' Chile." *HortScience*, 1993.

Bosland, Paul, Jaime Iglesias and Steve Tanksley. "'NuMex Conquistador' Paprika Pepper." *HortScience*, 1991.

———. "'NuMex Sunrise,' 'NuMex Sunset,' and 'NuMex Eclipse' Ornamental Chile Peppers." *HortScience*, 1990.

Burks, Thomas, Stephen Buck and Matthew Miller. "Mechanisms of Depletion of Substance P by Capsaicin." 1985.

Bustillos, Longino. "New Mexico: A Rich Cultural History of Farming and Ranching." USDA blog, September 10, 2014.

Cabeza, Fabiola. *The Good Life: New Mexico Traditions and Food*. Santa Fe: Museum of New Mexico Press, 2005.

Carleton, William. *The Expanding Ecology of a Hot Commodity: A Century of Changes in the New Mexico Chile Pepper*. Albuquerque: University of New Mexico, 2011.

Chilepepperinstitute.org. "The Story of Chile Peppers." 2007.

Chm.bris.ac.uk. "The Effect of Chillies on the Body" (accessed February 14, 2015).

Cocinas de New Mexico. Albuquerque, NM: Public Service Company of New Mexico, 1990.

Coggan, Catherine. "Chocolate Tortillas from Chimayó." *New Mexico Business Journal* (June 1, 1996).

Collins, Mayer-Wasmund, and Paul Bosland. "Improved Method for Quantifying Capsaicinoids in Capsicum Using High-Performance Liquid Chromatography." *HortScience*, 1995.

Coon, Danise, Eric Votava and Paul Bosland. *The Chile Cultivars of New Mexico State University Released from 1913 to 2008*. Las Cruces: New Mexico State University, Agricultural Experiment Station, 2008.

Creamland Dairies. "Creamland Dairies, Inc. History." http://www.creamland.com/history.shtml (accessed February 14, 2015).

DeWitt, Dave. *The Chile Pepper Encyclopedia: Everything You'll Ever Need to Know about Hot Peppers, with More than 100 Recipes*. New York: HarperCollins, 1999.

———. "College of Agricultural, Consumer and Environmental Sciences." *Resources* (Spring 2000).

———. *Dishing Up New Mexico: 145 Recipes from the Land of Enchantment*. North Adams, MA: Storey Publishing, 2014.

DeWitt, Dave, and Nancy Gerlach. *The Whole Chile Pepper Book*. New York: Little, Brown, 1990.

DeWitt, Dave, and Paul Bosland. *The Complete Chile Pepper Book: A Gardener's Guide to Choosing, Growing, Preserving, and Cooking*. Portland, OR: Timber Press, 2009.

DeWitt, Dave, Melissa Stock and Kellye Hunter. *The Healing Powers of Peppers: With Chile Pepper Recipes and Folk Remedies for Better Health and Living*. New York: Crown Publishing Group, 1998.

Discovery. "Milk Best Cure for Spice of Hot Chilies." April 11, 2012.

Eddins, Ned. "Southwest Indian Cultures." 2002. www.thefurtrapper.com.

Erowid, Earth, and Fire Erowid. "Hot Chiles: Surfing the Burn." *Erowid Extracts* (November 2004): 7:16–17.

Flint, Richard, and Shirley Flint. "Francisco Vázquez de Coronado." New Mexico Office of the State Historian, n.d.

Flores, Nancy. "Processing Fresh Chile Peppers." June 2005. Aces.nmsu.edu.

Ford, D'Lyn. "NMSU Scientists Release Ultra Red Chile Pepper." NMSU News Center, February 4, 2002.

Foster, Nelson. *Chilies to Chocolate: Food the Americas Gave the World*. Tucson: University of Arizona Press, 1992.

Fryxell, David. "The Red-or-Greening of New Mexico." December 2007. Desertexposure.com.

Garcia, Fabian. *Chile Culture*. Las Cruces: New Mexico College of Agriculture and Mechanic Arts, 1908.

———. *Improved Variety No. 9 of Native Chile*. Las Cruces: New Mexico State University Cooperative Extension Service, 1921.

Goldman, Jason. "On Capsaicin: Why Do We Love to Eat Hot Peppers?" *Scientific American* (November 30, 2011).

Harper, Roy. *An Improved Variety of Chile for New Mexico*. Las Cruces: New Mexico State University Agricultural Experiment Station, 1950.

———. *An Improved Variety of Chile for New Mexico*. Las Cruces: New Mexico State University Agricultural Experiment Station, 1967.

Hatch Chile Express. "Hatch Chile Express." http://www.hatch-chile.com/# (accessed February 14, 2015).

Hatch Chile Information. "Hatch Chile—The Real Story." http://www.zianet. com/focus (accessed February 14, 2015).

Hawkes, Jerry, James Libbin, and Brandon Jones. "Chile Production in New Mexico and Northern Mexico." *Journal of the A|S|F|M|R|A* (2008).

Hendricks, Rick. "Mr. Chile: Roy M. Nakayama." New Mexico Office of the State Historian, February 14, 2015.

Hobson, Jeremy. "Scientists Try to Bring Back the Original New Mexico Chile." *Here and Now*, November 17, 2014. Available online at http://hereandnow.wbur. org/2014/11/17/new-mexico-green-chiles.

Hughes, Phyllis. *Pueblo Indian Cookbook: Recipes from the Pueblos of the American Southwest*. Santa Fe: Museum of New Mexico Press, 1972.

Hultquist, Mike, and Patty Hultquist. "Chile Pepper Madness." http://www.chilipeppermadness.com (accessed February 14, 2015).

Kagel, Katharine. *Café Pasqual's Cookbook: Spirited Recipes from Santa Fe*. San Francisco, CA: Chronicle Books, 1993.

Kakawa Chocolate House. "Chili Chocolate." http://www.kakawachocolates.com/chili-chocolates.php (accessed February 14, 2015).

Las Cruces Chile Drop. "The First Las Cruces Chile Drop." http://www.lascruceschiledrop.com/home.html (accessed February 14, 2015).

Losee, Edgar. "Ancient Southwest Cultures." March 5, 2009. Redlandsfortnightly.org.

Los Poblanos Historic Inn & Organic Farm. "About." http://www.lospoblanos.com/about (accessed February 14, 2015).

Lutz, Fayne. "Cooking Northern New Mexico Traditional Foods." *Taos News*, 1989.

Masker, Mark. "Tropic Thunder: Hurricane Dave Hits the Sandia Resort." "Burn!" blog, March 6, 2014.

Matta, Frank, and Roy Nakayama. "'Espanola Improved' Chile Pepper." *HortScience*, 1984.

———. "'NuMex R Naky' Chile Pepper." *HortScience*, 1985.

McGraw, Kate. "Cafe Closure Leaves a Void in Chimayó." *Albuquerque Journal*, January 9, 2012.

McPhilomy, Janis. "Men Behind the Chile Pepper." *Borderlands*, 1991.

McQuaid, John. "Why We Love the Pain of Spicy Food." *Wall Street Journal*, December 31, 2014.

Mercola, Joseph. "How Chilies Can Be Used to Treat Pain." July 14, 2014. Mercola.com.

Montaño, Mary. *Tradiciones Nuevomexicanas: Hispano Arts and Culture of New Mexico*. Albuquerque: University of New Mexico Press, 2001.

Nabhan, Gary, Kraig Kraft and Kurt Friese. *Chasing Chiles: Hot Spots along the Pepper Trail*. White River Junction, VT: Chelsea Green Publishing, 2011.

Nakayama, Roy. *Notice of the Naming and Release of 'NuMex Big Jim,' a Semi-Mild Pungent Chile Variety for New Mexico*. Las Cruces: New Mexico State University Agricultural Experiment Station, 1975.

New Mexico Chile Association. "Get New Mexico Chile." http://www.getnmchile.com (accessed February 14, 2015).

New Mexico Chile Association Report, 2006.

New Mexico Commission of Public Records. "Our Mission & History." http://www.nmcpr.state.nm.us/archives/about-the-archives (accessed February 14, 2015).

New Mexico Genealogical Society. "Locating Catholic Church Records in New Mexico and Southern Colorado." http://www.nmgs.org/Churches.php?page=Churches.RecordsAndSources (accessed February 14, 2015).

New Mexico Office of the State Historian. "Spanish Colonial Period." http://newmexicohistory.org/historical-events-and-timeline/spanish-colonial (accessed February 14, 2015).

"New Mexico's Regional Chiles: Opportunities and Challenges in Place-Based Food Marketing." New Leaf AgDev Briefs, 2009.

New Mexico Tourism Department. "Food and Wine Events." http://www.newmexico.org/culinary-events (accessed February 14, 2015).

Niederman, Sharon. "New Mexico's Tasty Traditions: Recollections, Recipes and Photos." *New Mexico Magazine*, 2010.

"The Official Federal Land Records Site." http://www.glorecords.blm.gov/default.aspx (accessed February 14, 2015).

Padilla, Carmella. *The Chile Chronicles: Tales of a New Mexico Harvest*. Santa Fe: Museum of New Mexico Press, 1997.

Prescott, William. "History of the Conquest of Mexico, the Aztecs (Part Five)." 1992. http://history-world.org.

Raloff, Janet. "Understanding Why Hot Peppers Are Slimming." *Science News*, June 3, 2010.

Ramsey, David. "Some Like It Extra Hot." *Oxford American*, June 4, 2014.

Reeve, Frank. *History of New Mexico*. Vol. 1. Albuquerque: Center for Southwest Research, University Libraries, University of New Mexico, 1961.

Roberts, Scott, and Eric Vinje. "Chile Pepper Facts." Official Scott Roberts Website, May 31, 2014. http://www.scottrobertsweb.com/chile-pepper-facts.

Rohrig, Brian. "Hot Peppers: Muy Caliente!" American Chemical Society, December 1, 2013.

Rozin, Paul, and Deborah Schiller. "The Nature and Acquisition of a Preference for Chili Pepper by Humans." *Motivation and Emotion* 4, no. 1 (1980): 77–101.

Sais, James. *Making Chile Ristras*. Las Cruces: New Mexico State University Cooperative Extension Service, 1989.

Santa Fe New Mexican. "Leona Tiede Medina's Obituary." December 3, 2014.

Skaggs, Rhonda, Marcel Decker and Dawn VanLeeuwen. *A Survey of Southern New Mexico Chile Producers: Production Practices and Problems*. Las Cruces: New Mexico State University Agricultural Experiment Station, 2000.

Soular, Diana. "Amount of Chile Produced in New Mexico Continues to Drop." *Las Cruces Sun-News*, March 7, 2015.

———. "New Mexico Chile Acreage Hits Four-Decade Low." *Las Cruces Sun-News*, April 1, 2014.

Tepper, Rachel. "Thrill Seekers More Likely to Enjoy Spicy Foods, Research Suggests." *Huffington Post*, July 18, 2013.

"Timeline of New Mexico History." January 18, 2012. http://www.slideshare.net/jessshoe78/timeline-of-new-mexico-history.

Turner, Jack. *Spice: The History of a Temptation*. New York: Knopf Doubleday Publishing Group, 2004.

USDA National Agricultural Statistics Service. "2013 New Mexico Chile Production." http://www.nass.usda.gov/Statistics_by_State/New_Mexico/Publications/Chile/13-chile-release.pdf (accessed February 14, 2015).

Votava, Eric, Danise Coon, Colt Balok and Paul Bosland. "Inheritance of Unique Fruit and Foliage Color Mutation in 'NuMex Piñata.'" *Journal of Heredity* (2000).

Walker, Stephanie, Marisa Wall and Paul Bosland. "'NuMex Garnet' Paprika." *HortScience*, 2004.

Weigle, Marta, and Peter White. *The Lore of New Mexico*. Albuquerque: University of New Mexico Press, 2003.

Wikipedia. "Chili Pepper." http://en.wikipedia.org/wiki/Chili_pepper (accessed February 14, 2015).

———. "Terroir." http://en.wikipedia.org/wiki/Terroir (accessed February 14, 2015).

Williams, Clark. "Pepper Power." *ChemMatters*, April 1995.

Zewdie, Yayeh, Sharon Thomas and Paul Bosland. "'NuMex Nematador,' a Nematode Resistant Cayenne Chile." *HortScience*, 2003.

INDEX

ABOUT THE AUTHOR

As a filmmaker, Kelly Urig has a knack for creative storytelling and an eye for photography. Her films have won various awards and recognitions throughout the United States, but her true passion lies with food and its cultural, economic and historic importance. Kelly is also an avid photographer and took the majority of photos found in this book during her travels around New Mexico.

Photo by Jessica Clark.

Kelly earned her bachelor of arts degree from the University of Denver and received her master of arts in television, film and media production from San Diego State University. Kelly is a native of Santa Fe, New Mexico, and credits the unique culture and people of the state for her storytelling perspective.

For more chile adventures with Kelly, visit www.chilechica.com.

Visit us at
www.historypress.net

. . . .

This title is also available as an e-book